Landmarks of world literature

Albert Camus

THE STRANGER

Landmarks of world literature

General Editor: J. P. Stern

ALBERT CAMUS

The Stranger

PATRICK McCARTHY

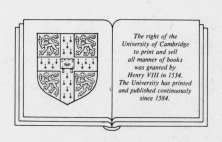

The right of the
University of Cambridge
to print and sell
all manner of books
was granted by
Henry VIII in 1534.
The University has printed
and published continuously
since 1584.

CAMBRIDGE UNIVERSITY PRESS

Cambridge
New York *New Rochelle* *Melbourne* *Sydney*

Published by the Press Syndicate of the University of Cambridge
The Pitt Building, Trumpington Street, Cambridge CB2 1RP
32 East 57th Street, New York, NY 10022, USA
10 Stamford Road, Oakleigh, Melbourne 3166, Australia

© Cambridge University Press 1988

First published 1988

Printed in Great Britain at
the University Press, Cambridge

British Library cataloguing in publication data

McCarthy, Patrick
Albert Camus, The stranger. −
(Landmarks of world literature).
I. Title   II. Series
843′.912   PQ2605.A3734E8

Library of Congress cataloguing in publication data

McCarthy, Patrick, 1941−
Albert Camus, The stranger.
(Landmarks of world literature)
Bibliography.
1. Camus, Albert, 1913−1960. Etranger.   I. Title.
II. Series.
PQ2605.A3734F838   1988   843′.914   87−27747

ISBN 0 521 32958 2 hard covers
ISBN 0 521 33851 4 paperback

Contents

Preface

This book is an examination of Camus's *The Stranger*, a work that is regarded as a twentieth-century classic. The main section, Chapter 2, begins with an analysis of the language of the novel, and then deals with the many problems posed by the narrative structure, the relationship between Part 1 and Part 2, and so on. Much has been written on *The Stranger* and this chapter is an attempt to synthesize existing interpretations. One theme has been singled out, namely, the treatment of the Arab, because it seems to me to have been somewhat neglected. But even here no attempt is made to offer a completely new reading.

The other chapters provide supplementary information. Chapter 1 begins with a biographical sketch of the young Camus and readers who believe that the link between a man and his work is unimportant, may prefer to skip it. The remainder of the chapter deals with the historical context − or more precisely the conflicting *contexts* − in which *The Stranger* may be set. Chapter 3 examines the parallels and contrasts between the novel and some of Camus's other early books; it also discusses the young Sartre. Chapter 4 summarizes the reasons why *The Stranger* is regarded as a classic, sets some of the criticism written on it in a historical context and makes suggestions for further reading.

An attempt has been made to write simply and without unnecessary jargon. All quotations have been translated into English by me and such translations have been kept as literal as possible. References to *The Stranger* are to the most accessible edition: *L'Etranger* (Paris: Gallimard, Folio, 1984). Other references to Camus's writing are to the two-volume Pléiade edition (Paris: Gallimard, 1972 and 1974) of his *Collected Works*. Titles are given in English wherever possible, except in Chapter 4 where precise bibliographical information is provided. In Chapter 2 references to other critical works have been kept as concise as possible in order not to burden the text. Complete references to all these works are given in Chapter 4.

L'Etranger is translated as *The Outsider* in the British version and as *The Stranger* in the US. The latter title has been adopted in this book because the term 'Outsider' has acquired cultural connotations that have nothing to do with Camus, whereas the term 'Stranger' is neutral.

I wish to express my gratitude to Valentin Mudimbé for reading Chapter 2 and to James Grieve for his comments on the Stuart Gilbert translation of the novel.

Washington DC   Patrick McCarthy

Chronology

	Camus's life and work	Literary events	Historical events
1902		Gide, *The Immoralist*.	
1912		Claudel, *Tidings Brought to Mary*.	
1913	C. born at Mondovi, Algeria.	Proust, *Swann's Way*	
1914	Father mortally wounded in Battle of the Marne.		Outbreak of First World War.
1919			Treaty of Versailles.
1926		Hemingway, *The Sun also Rises*.	
1930	First attack of tuberculosis.		Centenary of conquest of Algeria.
1932		Céline, *Journey to the End of the Night*.	
1933	Attends University of Algiers.	Malraux, *Man's Fate*.	Hitler becomes Chancellor of Germany.
1934	Marriage to Simone Hié.	James M. Cain, *The Postman always Rings Twice*	February riots by right-wing Leagues.
1935	Joins Communist Party.		Mussolini invades Abyssinia.
1936	Leaves university. Travels in Central Europe. Marriage breaks up. Starts theatre group.	Céline, *Death on the Instalment Plan*.	Remilitarization of the Rhineland. Popular Front to power. Spanish Civil War.

1937	Leaves Communist Party. Travels in Italy. Refuses teaching post in Sidi-Bel-Abbès. *Betwixt and Between*.	Arab nationalist protest organized in Algeria by Messali.
1938	Journalist at *Alger-Républicain*.	Malraux, *Man's Hope*. Sartre, *Nausea*. Nizan, *The Conspiracy*. Failure of Blum-Viollette plan to expand Arab franchise. Daladier forms government. Munich agreement.
1939	*Nuptials*. Articles on Kabylia.	Sartre, *The Wall*. Germany occupies Czechoslovakia. Franco's victory in Spain. Nazi–Soviet pact. Invasion of Poland.
1940	*Alger-Républicain* banned. Moves to Paris and works at *Paris-Soir*. Evacuation to Lyon. Marriage to Francine Faure.	German occupation of France. Vichy government established.
1941	Loses *Paris-Soir* post. Returns to Oran.	Hitler invades Soviet Union.
1942	Illness forces C. to return to France and convalesce in Massif Central. *The Stranger* and *The Myth of Sisyphus*.	Ponge, *The Voice of Things*. Allied invasion of North Africa. German occupation of Southern France.

1943	Moves to Paris. Reader at Gallimard. Meeting with Sartre. Winter 1943/4: journalist at resistance newspaper, *Combat*. Meeting with Maria Casarès.	Sartre, *Being and Nothingness* and *The Flies*. Malraux joins Resistance.	Italian surrender. Growth of Resistance.
1944	*Cross Purpose*. C. and Pia run the now legal *Combat*.	Céline flees France to avoid trial as collaborator. Sartre, *No Exit*.	Allied landings in Normandy. Liberation of Paris. Ho Chi Minh proclaims independence of Vietnam.
1945	C. visits Algeria. Articles attacking French policy. Birth of twins – Jean and Catherine. First performance of *Caligula*.	Sartre, *The Age of Reason*.	Armistice. Sétif massacre in Algeria. Bombing of Hiroshima.
1946	Visit to United States.		
1947	Leaves *Combat*. *The Plague*.	Malraux joins Gaullists.	De Gaulle resigns. Communists leave government. Marshall Aid. Rebellion in Madagascar.
1948	*State of Siege*. Resumes love affair with Maria Casarès.	Sartre, *What is Literature?* and *Dirty Hands*.	Prague Communist coup.

Year			
1949	Visit to South America. Renewed tuberculosis. *The Just.*		Signing of North Atlantic Treaty.
1950	Convalescence at Grasse.		Korean War.
1951	*The Rebel.*	Gide's death.	
1952	Quarrel with Sartre.	Sartre, *Communists and Peace.* Céline, *Fairytale for Another Time.*	Ridgway riots/Cold War worsens.
1953	Wife ill, C. depressed and unable to write. Director at Angers theatre festival.	Barthes, *Writing, Zero Degree.* Robbe-Grillet, *The Erasers.*	
1954	*Summer.*		Fall of Dien Bien Phu. Mendès France government. Algerian War breaks out.
1955	Visit to Greece. Articles for *Express.*		
1956	Visit to Algiers and appeal for truce. Withdrawal from *Express.* Illness and depression. Separation from wife. *The Fall.*	Sarraute, *The Age of Suspicion.* Céline, *Castle to Castle.*	Independence of Morocco and Tunisia recognized. Suez invasion. Intensified fighting in Algeria. Budapest uprising.
1957	*Exile and Kingdom. Caligula* performed at Angers. Nobel prize. Controversy over Algerian War.	Robbe-Grillet, *Jealousy.*	

1958	*Actuelles III*: C's articles on Algeria. Buys house at Lourmarin in Southern France.	Simone de Beauvoir, *Memoirs of a Dutiful Daughter*.	Revolt of army and French-Algerians. De Gaulle returns to power. Fifth Republic established.
1959	Adapts and directs Dostoyevsky's *The Possessed*. Working on novel, *The First Man*.	Malraux becomes Minister of Culture.	
1960	4 January: killed in car accident at Villeblevin.	Sartre, *Critique of Dialectical Reason*.	French-Algerian revolt against De Gaulle.

Chapter 1

Contexts

Biographical sketch

When *The Stranger* was published in 1942 Albert Camus was 29 years old. He was born a year before the outbreak of the First World War and his father was killed in the early battles. A semi-autobiographical essay recounts that Camus's mother kept a piece of the shell that had been taken from her husband's body and exhibited his medals in their living-room. Unsurprisingly, Camus grew up with a horror of war that led him to oppose French re-armament throughout the 1930's. The psychological effects of his father's death are harder to explain, but in his life Camus sought the friendship of older men like Jean Grenier and Pascal Pia, while in *The Stranger* the father makes one intriguing appearance.

The young Camus was drawn all the closer to his mother who brought him up in the working-class Algiers district of Belcourt where she earned her living cleaning houses. Uneducated, overworked and withdrawn, Catherine Sintès was a complex influence on her son. In his public statements Camus insisted on his attachment to her, declaring that he wished to place at the centre of his writing her 'admirable silence' (*Preface to Betwixt and Between*, OC 2,13). This silence was a sign of stoicism, a rudimentary form of the in-difference that is a key concept in his writing, and a warning against the falsity inherent in literary discourse.

The same essay calls the silence of the mother 'animal' and depicts her as cold: 'she never caressed her son because she wouldn't know how to' (*Betwixt and Between*, OC 2,25). The denial of affection haunts the narrator who tells a disturbing anecdote about a mother cat eating her kitten. Conversely, the essay depicts an assault on the mother by an intruder, after which the narrator-son spends the night next to her on her bed.

A simple psychoanalytic reading would lead one to conclude that Camus was torn between an incestuous love for his mother and a hostility towards her coldness. Neither feeling could be avowed and each could inspire guilt. The mother is a problematic figure in his writing: in *The Stranger* she is, at least superficially, spurned, while in *The Plague* Rieux's mother replaces his wife. Camus's dealings with women were shaped by his mother and, although he moved out of their Belcourt flat before he left grammar school, the bond they shared endured until his death.

Poverty was associated with her and constituted another influence. Camus's family belonged to the poorer segment of the working class and most of his relatives were labourers or artisans. He was able to attend grammar school and university only because he obtained scholarships, and he did not need to read Marx in order to appreciate the importance of class. As a student, and later, he supported himself by giving lessons or by tedious office jobs. When he travelled he had to eat in the cheapest restaurants and buy excursion tickets that could not be used on the most convenient trains.

This too is reflected in his books. He has moments of tearful sentimentality when he depicts Salamano's dog in *The Stranger* or the figure of Grand in *The Plague*. But more frequently his working-class background inspires him with a caustic view of the universe: jobs are hard work rather than careers, while ideals are hypocrisy or veiled forms of oppression. *The Stranger* strips the legal system and the French state of their legitimacy.

Yet working-class life was also a source of happiness to Camus. It was carefree, and in Belcourt there was a comradeship which he missed years later when he was a Parisian celebrity. He loved Algiers streetlife: the swagger of the boys and the unashamed sexuality of the girls. In *The Stranger* Marie is very much the working-class woman in her enjoyment of her own body. Moreover, Camus saw a moral code in Belcourt: honesty, loyalty and pride were values that were lived rather than imposed.

In 1930 Camus had his first attack of tuberculosis. He

never fully recovered and the disease returned regularly throughout his life. Characteristically, he rarely spoke of it, although it was all the graver because it was badly understood at the time. Treatment consisted of injecting air into the damaged lung in order to collapse it and give it time to heal; Camus endured this as well as fits of coughing and spitting up blood. Tuberculosis must surely have sharpened his sense of death and, conversely, his appreciation of the human body as a fountain of strength and grace. It put an end to a promising career as a soccer player, although Camus continued to love sport and to spend long hours on the Algiers beaches.

One cannot help feeling that, despite the huge success he would enjoy after the publication of *The Stranger* and *The Plague*, Camus's life was a bleak one, and it was rendered still bleaker by his marriage while still a university student to Simone Hié. Beautiful, intelligent and from an unconventional family, Simone, whom Camus loved deeply, was a hopeless drug addict. During the two years of their married life together — 1934 to 1936 — she battled against her addiction and Camus, drawing on the courage he deployed against tuberculosis, helped her. It was to no avail and their separation caused him much distress.

Here again one must not exaggerate for, if Camus's life was a struggle, he won many victories. He emerged from the university with his degree and an additional 'diplôme d'études supérieures'; he had as mentor Jean Grenier, his philosophy teacher, who was an accomplished writer published by the house of Gallimard, and he had a wide circle of friends. Young people, mostly from the university of Algiers, usually interested in painting, sculpture or the theatre, flocked to him and were almost unanimous in accepting him as a leader. Women were drawn by his good looks as well as his blend of moral integrity and irony. Camus had a flair for being happy, and the reader recalls how memories of happiness come flooding over Meursault while he is in prison.

Aware from his adolescence that he wanted to be a writer, Camus tried his hand at philosophy, essays, fiction and the theatre. From 1936 on he had his own theatre group which put on plays that he directed. Like many mainland French artists, he felt that the French theatre was in the doldrums, ruined by bedroom comedies and well-made plays that left the audience amused but otherwise unmoved. Camus's productions were designed to jolt the spectator, alternatively drawing him into the work and isolating him from it.

In an adaptation of André Malraux's book *The Time of Scorn* the audience became the spectators at the trial of the German Communist Thälmann and at the end they were persuaded to join in the singing of the *Internationale*. In *Asturian Revolt*, co-authored by Camus but never performed in full because it was banned by the right-wing municipality of Algiers, the audience became the crowds on the street during an uprising by Spanish miners. Conversely, during Aeschylus's *Prometheus in Chains* the actors wore masks to prevent the audience from identifying with them, while a loudspeaker poured forth philosophical discourse. This time the break with theatrical convention made the spectators brood on the concept of revolt.

It is possible to detect in this an echo of Bert Brecht's theatre with its emphasis on what is often called 'alienation effect'. Camus was fascinated by the edge of distance that the actor brings to his role and, when he played Ivan in a production of Dostoyevsky's *Karamazov*, he was remote and silent while the other actors scampered frenetically around him. In general, however, Camus did not think highly of Brecht's methods and preferred the opposite pole of greater audience involvement. The scenery for his productions was stylized to create a mood, while the lighting and sound effects were over- rather than under-stated.

It is nonetheless intriguing that Jean Grenier, who had seen these productions, should recognize in *The Stranger* a 'distance' which he had perceived in Camus's theatrical experiments (Jean Grenier, 'A work, a man', *Cahiers du Sud*, February 1943, p. 228). Moreover, the chapter on acting in *The Myth of Sisyphus* deals with the actor's awareness that he is pretending to be what he is not. Camus's first and best play, *Caligula*, was first drafted for his group, and its hero displays both a frenzy of emotion and the knowledge that he is acting out a part for the city of Rome.

Asturian Revolt had a political dimension because Camus was an energetic left-wing militant who was active in the anti-Fascist struggle. In 1935 he joined the Communist Party, which was then expanding and moving towards the policy of the Popular Front. His task was to organize cultural activities with a political slant: at the Algiers House of Culture he showed Russian films, ran debates and supported Arab protest movements. He found an audience drawn from students, trade union supporters and the left-wing segments of the middle classes.

In 1937 Camus left the Communist Party for several reasons, the chief of which was the party's failure to defend Arab nationalists who had been jailed by the French government. This should not, however, lead one to suppose that Camus — or any other French – Algerian — supported Algerian independence. His criticism of the party was more moral than political: it had not extended a hand to friends who needed help. Camus remained an active left-winger and in October 1938 he started work as a journalist for *Alger – Républicain*, a newspaper that was founded to support the Popular Front and that had as editor the fiercely independent Pascal Pia.

By now he had begun writing *The Stranger*, but before discussing the development of the novel one might turn to the history of the period, which would shape both the book and the way it was received. One must glance at French literary and political history and then at the very different situation of Algeria. Indeed the special traits of *The Stranger* emerge from the contradictions between the two sets of contexts.

Historical contexts

Jean Grenier encouraged Camus to immerse himself in the writing of the *Nouvelle Revue Française*. Proust, Gide and others had dominated the 1920s, Gallimard had become the leading literary publishing house and the *NRF* the leading magazine. In so far as it is possible to define in a few lines a complex body of writing, the *NRF* group may be said to uphold the integrity of inner life. Gide maintained that man could liberate himself from family, tradition and a morality of self-interest in order to discover his other, more sincere self. From Proust's novel one might draw the lesson that, if human experience is fragmentary, there are moments when involuntary memory or intuition creates a totality. Similarly Paul Claudel's version of Catholicism emphasized that, if man was miserable and incomplete, he could transcend himself by taking up the dialogue with a God who was jealous and severe but not absent.

By the 1930s some of these tenets were coming under fire. The slaughter in the trenches had undercut Gide's view of life as an adventure, while the depression and the rise of Fascism strengthened the mood of pessimism. Individual psychology seemed less important than the general human condition, the theme of death took brutal forms, and freedom became an urgent need to act. Politics entered writing and the debate about commitment was keen.

The two writers who most influenced the generation of Camus and Sartre were André Malraux and Louis-Ferdinand Céline. Malraux's *Man's Fate* (1933) expounded the view that man must confront his mortality and give meaning to his existence by engaging in political action. The new hero is 'Bolshevik man' – the band of Chinese revolutionaries in the novel – who has fewer rights than duties. His duty lies to the revolution, which is depicted as a struggle that transforms the militant's life by letting him participate in a movement that not merely liberates the working class, but assures him some sort of immortality.

Camus was an admirer of Malraux, who had been friendly with Jean Grenier and who would be one of the readers when *The Stranger* was submitted to Gallimard. But if Camus drew from Malraux the concern for values such as courage, lucidity and virility, the differences between the two men are also great. The chapter on conquest in *The Myth of Sisyphus* may be read as a critique of the mystique of revolution that is found in *Man's Fate*.

Céline exerted no influence on Camus and one may note only that, while his attempt to construct a new language based on Parisian slang, obscenities and lyricism is light-years from the concision of *The Stranger*, it is a very different solution to the same problem. Where the *NRF* had believed — albeit not simplistically — in language and in the integrity of the work of art, Céline and Camus criticize traditional literary discourse and the notion that the novel creates a harmonious universe.

Diverse foreign influences were present in the 1930s. Nietzsche remained important as he had been since the turn of the century, and so did Dostoyevsky. German phenomenology was a more recent import and Sartre studied Husserl — who is also discussed in *The Myth of Sisyphus* — in an attempt to combat what he perceived as the shallow rationalism of the Cartesian tradition. This was the period when American novelists such as Faulkner, Dos Passos and Hemingway were translated, although the question of their direct influence is complex, and attempts to link *The Stranger* with Hemingway may be misleading.

So the concepts of the absurd and of Existentialism, which came into French writing in the late 1930s and which are associated with the names of Camus and Sartre, draw on a mood of nihilism. The parallels and — more importantly — the differences between the two men are discussed in Chapter 3, but here one may note that coming from very different backgrounds they arrived at a similar critique of traditional values. Sartre was in flight from his middle-class, educated family and excoriated pretention. As Simone de Beauvoir puts it, he and his friends 'derided every inflated idealism, laughed to scorn delicate souls, noble souls, all souls and any kind of souls, inner life itself . . . they affirmed that men were not spirits but bodies exposed to physical needs' (Simone de Beauvoir, *Memoirs of a Dutiful Daughter* (Paris: Gallimard 1958), p. 335).

From his working-class upbringing Camus learned to be similarly suspicious of ideals, to be sceptical of reason and introspection, and to believe that the coherent self and the coherent work of art were fabrications. Along with this went the realization that life was to be lived rather than dreamed about or mulled over. Man existed, so Existentialism maintained, among or *against* others in a brutal adventure, to which he must by his actions give meaning.

Camus and Sartre would not have exerted such influence if they had not been flanked by other writers, each different but sharing common themes. Francis Ponge's poetry offers parallels with Sartre in its treatment of objects; Maurice Blanchot's concept of anguish may be compared and contrasted with Camus's sense of the absurd; the arguments about language were foreshadowed in the work of Jean Paulhan, the editor of the *NRF*, and would soon be taken up by Roland Barthes.

The mood of pessimism was encouraged by political developments. Camus was not 20 when Hitler came to power in Germany; he then lived through Mussolini's invasion of Abyssinia (1935), Hitler's remilitarization of the Rhineland (1936) and Franco's rebellion in Spain (1936). If these were good enough causes for gloom, they also galvanized the Left. The riots of February 1934, when right-wing extremists seemed to be attempting a coup d'état in France, helped unite the French Left and led to the Popular Front victory in the elections of April 1936.

As the decade wore on, the Left's defeats grew more numerous: Léon Blum, the Popular Front's prime minister, fell from power in June 1937; in September 1938 came the Munich agreement, and the next year the Republicans were defeated in Spain. This was a painful blow to Camus, who was proud that his mother's family was Spanish. By now the drift towards war was apparent, even if Camus fought stubbornly against it.

The mood of malaise and drifting, as well as the sense of having no guidelines except those one could invent for oneself, finds its way into Camus's early writing, which has usually been read as a reflection of the conflicts in France and in Europe. But the other context was making itself felt: French-Algeria was going through torments of its own.

When Camus was 17 French-Algeria celebrated its centenary and it seemed to everyone, including Camus, that the conquest was safe for ever. Certainly there were only 900,000 Europeans alongside 6 million Arabs, but open Arab revolt had ended in the previous century and the military parades for the centenary emphasized French power. However, economic difficulties increased in the 1930s because of the agricultural slump, and many Arab farmers lost their land. They came flooding into the cities and Camus noted an increase of them in his own Belcourt.

This was a source of tension, and Arab protest grew. Islam was a rallying point, and the ulemas or Moslem doctors offered a stricter, purified version of their religion. Arab politicians pressed for reforms within the context of French rule and of the ideology of assimilation. The absurdity of assimilation was apparent: officially Arabs were equal and were eventually to enjoy all the rights of French citizenship; however, in the meantime they were treated like a conquered population. Yet the Popular Front included in its platform the Blum – Viollette plan to widen – very moderately – the Arab franchise. After the Front's failure to enact the plan, a radical group of Arabs led by Messali Hadj edged towards nationalism. An ex-Communist who had believed the party line that the colonial struggle was part of the international struggle of the proletariat, Messali was making a change of great significance.

The depression did not spare the French-Algerian or pied-noir community and heightened its contradictory view of France. French interests lay less in developing industry in Algeria than in exporting raw materials to be processed in France. Standards of living were lower in Algeria than in France, so the pied-noir's need for the protection of the French army jostled with his economic recriminations. This mixture of dislike and admiration is a theme in *The Stranger*, where Meursault and Marie have sharply differing attitudes towards Paris. The conflict between mother country and colony overlapped with a tension within the colony between the wealthy businessmen and farmers and the mass of the population.

In all this the crucial element was the pied-noir working class which was most threatened by cheap Arab labour and hence in greatest need of French protection, but which also suffered most from the existing economic order. This is the key group in *The Stranger*, the group to which Meursault belongs and from whose viewpoint he undermines the legitimacy of French institutions. At the same time the incident where he kills the Arab without understanding what he is doing is surely an expression of the violence that lay beneath the surface of assimilation.

Similarly *The Stranger*, which may be read in the context of the absurd and of Existentialism, is also a piece of pied-noir writing. Camus drew on the ways in which the French-Algerians depicted themselves; the myths they invented recur and are scrutinized in his novel.

Through French-Algerian writing and popular culture runs the motif of the pieds-noirs as a new nation. Half-European and half-African, they are a frontier people; they are pagans as well as unintellectual barbarians; the men are virile and the women sexy; they live through their bodies and are devoted to sport; temperamentally they oscillate between indolence and frenzied emotion. Camus elaborates on this view in the essays, *Nuptials* (1939), where he writes of Algeria: 'There is nothing here for the man who wishes to learn, get an education or improve. This country offers no lessons. It does not promise or hint. It is content to give in abundance . . . you know it as soon as you start to enjoy it' (*OC* 2,67).

In this it is easy to recognize the figure of Meursault, who shuns introspection and is devoted to sensuous experience. Equally obviously Camus has deepened the concept of indifference, which in Meursault is an unexplained mixture of inability to feel and protest against inauthentic emotion.

The murder of the Arab may also be placed in this context. French-Algerian portrayals of the Arab dissolve the colonial relationship into the brotherhood of pied-noir and Arab as fellow frontiersmen, or into the Mediterranean medley of French, Spanish, Maltese and Arabs living together on the fringes of Europe and Africa. The Arab intrigues the colonizer: he is nomadic, steeped in Islamic fatalism, different from the European and hence akin to the pied-noir. Once more Camus draws on previous depictions in *Betwixt and Between*, where the reflections on the mother, which have been quoted already, take place in an Arab café while the narrator sits alone with the owner. Silent, crouched in a corner and 'seeming to look at my now empty glass' (*OC* 2,24), the Arab incarnates indifference. He is thus linked with the mother, whose special indifference haunts Camus and is the origin of Meursault's indifference in *The Stranger*. In the novel Camus criticizes the pied-noir view by showing how violence can emerge from the kinship that the French-Algerian chooses to discover between himself and the Arab. Meursault and the Arab are rivals as well as brothers.

Camus dealt with Arab issues in the pages of *Alger-Républicain*. He campaigned for a French civil servant who had got into trouble for protecting Arab farmers, and he defended an Arab spokesman accused of murder. His best-known articles depicted the agricultural crisis in the Kabylia mountains and attacked the inadequacy of French social policy: the lack of schools and medical care. Camus called for government spending to build roads and provide water; then, entering the dangerous political arena, he demanded more self-government for local Arab communities. At this point he could go no further, because the next question would be why the French authorities did so little to help Kabylia and the only answer would be that, to the government and especially to French-Algerians, local self-government for Arabs interfered with colonial exploitation. The striking feature of Camus's articles is that they lead so clearly to this conclusion, which he does not draw.

For those who believe that biography is of any use in interpreting a novel, it is hard to imagine that the author of these pieces could have chosen to write a novel where an Arab is murdered, without brooding on his choice of victim. For those − a larger group − who believe a work must be set in its historical context or contexts, it is difficult to divorce the murder of the Arab from the deepening crisis of French-

Algeria. Not that Camus could speak openly of colonial violence but, unlike a newspaper article, a work of fiction can hint — in spite of itself — at forbidden topics.

By 1939, however, the other set of contexts was reasserting itself. *Alger-Républicain* conducted a vigorous campaign against the war, even after it had begun. While refusing to accept the Nazi occupation of Poland, Camus argued that concessions could be made in the corridor; he repeated that the Treaty of Versailles was unjust, he called on the Allies to offer peace, and he placed hope in Neville Chamberlain. The newspaper ran into troubles with the military censorship and it appeared with blanks, which amused Camus and Pia. Finally in January 1940 it was banned.

The Stranger and the war

Having no job, Camus left Algeria in March. He went to Paris, where Pia had found him a job on a sensational paper, *Paris-Soir*, not as a journalist but doing lay-out and copy-editing. It was a lonely, dreary time and he moved from one cheap hotel to another, homesick for Algeria. In June the staff of *Paris-Soir* fled just before the Germans entered Paris, Camus carrying the manuscript of *The Stranger* which he had provisionally finished in May.

The novel was only one of the projects at which he worked during these years. His earliest published works were the essays of *Betwixt and Between* and *Nuptials* (1937 and 1939). He also wrote a novel called *A Happy Death*, which he did not attempt to get published and which did not appear until long after his death. The relationship between *A Happy Death* and *The Stranger* is complex, and critics have wondered whether the former might be considered a trial run for the latter. For some time in 1937 and 1938 Camus worked at both novels, but by 1939 he had left *A Happy Death* and was pushing ahead with *The Stranger*. He also had a first draft of *Caligula* and was working on *The Myth of Sisyphus*.

In his mind these three works constituted the cycle of the absurd and went together, although *Caligula*, which he rewrote in 1939, went through further redrafting after *The Stranger* and *The Myth* were completed. Camus carried all three works around with him during the peregrinations of 1940; he finished the first half of *The Myth* in September and the second half in February 1941.

By then his life had changed again. *Paris-Soir* set up operations in Clermont-Ferrand and then in Lyon. On 3 December 1940 Camus was married to Francine Faure whom he had known in Algiers. Almost immediately he lost his job as *Paris-Soir* reduced its staff, and he decided to return to Algeria. Francine's family had a house in Oran where Camus could hope to get some part-time teaching. It was a difficult period: the Germans still appeared to have won the war and Camus had few career prospects, but at least he was going back to Algeria.

Although supposedly completed, *The Stranger* seems to have undergone a revision during this year. At all events a version was sent by Camus in Oran to Pia in Lyon in April 1941 (Herbert Lottman, *Albert Camus, a Biography* (New York: Doubleday 1979), p. 249). Pia sent it to Malraux, and on his and other recommendations the book was accepted for publication by Gallimard.

Since French publishers were working under an agreement between their federation and the German Propaganda-Staffel, the issue of censorship arose. Gaston Gallimard showed *The Stranger* to a representative of the Occupation authorities, who felt it contained nothing damaging to the German cause. When the book appeared in June 1942 two copies were sent − as with each new book − to the Propaganda-Staffel. When it was *The Myth*'s turn, it did not escape unscathed, for the chapter on Kafka was taken out: presumably Camus and/or Gallimard felt the Germans might not tolerate the study of a Jewish writer. Only then was the essay submitted to the authorities and published in December 1942.

Since *The Stranger*'s first edition consisted of a mere 4,400 copies, it could not become a best-seller. But it was well-received − the Propaganda-Staffel had made a mistake − in anti-Nazi circles, and Sartre's article, which is discussed later, helped launch Camus. In August 1942 he returned to France because his tuberculosis had flared up, and he was obliged to spend time in the Massif Central mountains at a village called Le Panelier. When the Allies invaded North Africa he was cut off from his wife and had to remain in France. He had little money, his health was bad and his diaries record his gloom.

These are the contexts which helped shape *The Stranger*'s success. A historical contradiction is involved because the novel, which springs from pre-war Algeria, was read during the dreary days of the Occupation. One should not exaggerate the contradiction because, as has already been argued, it was Camus's working-class and Algerian background which led him to the themes that struck a chord in the Paris of 1942, namely, the illegitimacy of authority and the primacy of concrete, individual experience. Yet the specifically Algerian features – the depiction of a pied-noir hero and the Arab problem – were generally overlooked, while *The Stranger* was read in a supposedly universal but in fact Western European context, as a manual of how an individual may live in a world without authentic values.

The Myth reinforced this and Camus became – quite deservedly – a great French and European writer of the 1940s. The language of *The Stranger*, which is suspicious of abstractions, exaggerations and itself, was a welcome antidote to the flowery rhetoric of the Vichy government, as well as a recognizable landmark in contemporary French prose.

Chapter 2

The Stranger

Meursault's languages

The very first paragraph of the novel poses the issue of language:

Aujourdhui, maman est morte. Ou peut-être hier, je ne sais pas. J'ai reçu un télégramme de l'asile: 'Mère décédée. Enterrement demain. Sentiments distingués.' Cela ne veut rien dire. C'était peut-être hier. (Mother died today. Or perhaps yesterday, I don't know. I received a telegram from the home: 'Your mother passed away. Funeral tomorrow. Sincerely yours.' That doesn't mean anything. Perhaps it was yesterday.) (9)

Two different kinds of language are juxtaposed as the narrator, an unidentified 'I', reads a text sent by 'the home' which is, as we later learn, an organ of the state. The telegram employs a euphemism, 'passed away', and ends with a purely formal greeting. It informs the reader of the event of his mother's death while concealing the significance of that death. It is also a command which the narrator-character obeys by departing to attend the funeral.

The narrator-reader does not, however, accept the telegram's authority without criticism. It 'doesn't mean anything', he notes; its langauge is unsatisfactory. By depicting the narrator as a reader, *The Stranger* is indicating to us, its own readers, how we should tackle it: we should be wary of the traps and commands it contains.

As for the narrator's own language, which surrounds and besieges the telegram, it is less formal, and uses the familiar French term 'maman' for 'mère'. It too conceals the reality of death, leaving open the question whether the narrator-character is troubled or not. But this language broadcasts its own inadequacy by the use of phrases like 'perhaps' and 'I don't know'.

This enables us to define the relationship between the telegram's language and the narrator's. The former is authoritative, sure of itself and closed to outside intervention; it does not tell us when the mother died, but it does inform us that it was itself composed 'today'. However, the latter is aware of an imprecision which it seeks unsuccessfully to correct. The two are in conflict and, although the narrator-character obeys the telegram, the narrator-reader fights back by turning it into a text written by himself.

One critic has stated that the telegram is 'the quintessence of writing', because it imposes abstract, arbitrary categories on the flux of human experience (Eisenzweig, p. 11). Certainly the written language is an instrument of oppression in *The Stranger*: the narrator, whom we discover to be a French-Algerian called Meursault (first name unknown), helps bring about the murder of an Arab by writing a deceitful letter to his sister. Moreover, Camus emphasizes that this is writing by omitting the content of the letter but describing the tools that Meursault uses to compose it: the 'squared paper', the 'small red wooden penholder' and the 'inkpot with purple ink' (54).

Yet the same critic, Uri Eisenzweig, points out that the problem of language is not to be resolved by a simple distinction between the written and the spoken. In the second half of the novel the language of oppression is the rhetoric of the courtroom contained in passages like this one: 'Who is the criminal here and what are these methods which consist of denigrating the prosecution witnesses in order to belittle their evidence which nonetheless remains overwhelming?' (139). The pseudo-question which imposes its own answer, the facile antithesis between 'belittle' ('minimiser') and 'overwhelming' ('écrasants') and the scarcely veiled assumption that the man in the dock is a criminal are the signs of a language that seeks to manipulate feelings rather than to reason. This is the spoken language, albeit linked with a privileged social class.

Conversely the narrator's language is not presented as conversational French. In the first paragraph both the 'ne' and the 'pas' are employed to form the negative, although authors who seek to present their novels as spoken, working-class

French almost always omit the 'ne'. Moreover, the language of the Algiers streets can, where it does occur, be a vehicle of oppression. The incident where Raymond beats up the Arab man is presented not by the narrator but by Raymond who uses slangy French. Significantly, this is the longest piece of conversational French in the book.

If the written/spoken categories are too simple, it remains true that there is a language of authority that is associated with the warden of the home, Meursault's boss and the law courts, and hence with the state and with economic and political power. There is, however, no working-class discourse that offers instant liberation from them (if there were, *The Stranger* would be an extremely poor novel). In the courtroom the working-class characters like Marie and Céleste are enmeshed in the language of authority and unable to make themselves understood. But, even as the court laughs at them because they cannot express themselves, the reader knows it is their inability to wield language that is the mark of their honesty.

Similarly, the note of dissidence in the narrator's language comes from its wariness. 'My case was taking its course, to borrow the judge's expression' ('selon l'expression même du juge') (110), notes Meursault. He will use the language of officialdom, but only while designating it as such; thus he is reminding us that Céleste would have put things differently, and that he himself is not presenting the statement as true. Indeed there is a minor character called Masson who adds 'I shall say more' to his utterances, so that the reader can never forget he is dealing with unreliable words rather than with stable objects.

The conflict between the languages of authority and dissidence is present in the first half of the book and dominates the second half. There, the true nature of authority is revealed at the end of Part 2, Chapter 4, when the judge 'said in a bizzare way that my head would be cut off in a public place in the name of 'the French people' (164). The pompous mention of 'the French people' is characteristic of what one might also call the language of the guillotine but, by noting it as such — 'in a bizzare way' — and by mocking it, Meursault the narrator revenges the defeat of Meursault the character.

These are not the only two languages of *The Stranger*, for the last chapter of Part 2 is written differently: one half of it as a rigorous intellectual meditation and the other half as a cry of revolt. The latter is the second cry, the first being the outburst of the Arab woman whom Raymond beats up. Each of them represents a visceral and partially non-verbal language which cuts through the falsity of language by its emotional intensity, and stands as a metaphor of true or total language. One cannot resist drawing the comparison with the primal scream. Another metaphor of totality is the monologue which Meursault conducts in prison. This is depicted as a stream of consciousness that enables him to hold onto an identity even as prison life is driving him towards schizophrenia. But, while he can tell the reader about this monologue, he cannot narrate it and its role is to emphasize the shortcomings of the diary or journal which constitutes *The Stranger*.

At the opposite pole from the cry and the monologue stands an equally impossible solution to the problem of language: silence. Certain social groups are forced into silence, which is hence associated with oppression; the Arabs barely speak at all. Yet since the Arabs do not themselves oppress, their silence is a mark of authenticity. Meursault the character is frequently silent: when questioned by the magistrate, he responds that 'the truth is I never have much to say. So I keep quiet' (104). Here again his taciturnity throughout his trial is presented as a protest against the wordiness of the lawyers.

Although the narrator of a novel can hardly be silent, he can introduce into his tale the awareness that silence contains authenticity. Meursault does this in the first paragraph by the brevity of his sentences and by the absence of subordinate clauses which imply causality and hierarchy. Not surprisingly, Roland Barthes concluded that the language of *The Stranger* 'exists as a silence' (Barthes, *Degré zéro*, p. 110).

We have by now moved from the antithesis authority/

dissidence, which does not furnish convincing explanations of the first half of the novel, to the antithesis totality/wariness. At the two key moments of Part 1 — the funeral of the mother in Chapter 1 and the killing of the Arab in Chapter 6 — the text discards wariness, as the following passage reveals:

Autour de moi c'était toujours la même campagne lumineuse gorgée de soleil. L'éclat du ciel était insoutenable . . . Le soleil avait fait éclater le goudron. Les pieds y enfonçaient et laissaient ouverte sa pulpe brillante. Au-dessus de la voiture le chapeau du cocher, en cuir bouilli, semblait avoir été pétri dans cette boue noire. J'étais un peu perdu entre le ciel bleu et blanc et la monotonie de ces couleurs, noir gluant du goudron ouvert, noir terne des habits, noir laqué de la voiture (Around me was always the same countryside gorged with sun. The glare from the sky was unbearable . . . The sun had burst open the tar on the road. Our feet sank into it and left its shiny pulp showing. Above the hearse the coachman's hat in molten leather seemed to have been moulded out of this black mud. I was a bit lost between the blue and white sky and the monotony of this colour, the sticky black of the open tar, the dull black of the clothes, the polished black of the hearse.) (29)

The words 'always' and 'same' indicate the suspension of time whether measured by months and years (as the state usually means it) or by yesterday and today (as Meursault measures it). The passage begins with sense impressions — the heat of the sun and the colour of the tar — but these trigger images of a battle. Changes of shape take place: the sun turns the road into a sticky pulp while the coachman's hat is dissolved into tar. This is a violent process and the real object of the assault by the sun is Meursault, who enters a hallucination where his sense of external reality and hence of himself starts to break down. Colours cease to be merely sensory and become obsessive: blue, which is associated throughout *The Stranger* with happiness, lingers but black, which is the colour of mourning and of the mother, overwhelms him.

Although Meursault retains a degree of control — the coachman's hat merely 'seemed' to be black mud — this passage shows how he loses his ability to measure space and time and becomes a part of the universe — his feet 'sank' into the mud. This is not the scientific universe but it is coherent in its colour structures, it has its organizing principle in the sun and it is consistent in its hostility to humans.

Such passages abound in Camus's work, and how one interprets them depends largely on which brand of explanations one favours — religious, psychoanalytical and so on. Several such explanations will be attempted later in this study. Sometimes these passages relate to joyous experiences, but in *The Stranger* they are often terrifying; nature (which is an elusive concept in Camus) can welcome and embrace man, but here she seeks to annihilate him.

It is obvious that this language is very different from the language of dissidence and that it has some of the attributes of poetry. Natural forces — the sun, sea, sand and rocks — are personified. Physical sensations are at first noted, but then turn into a flood of independent images. The narrator no longer undercuts himself, and he seems less to be narrating than to be transcribing a language that is forced upon him.

To explain the role of this other, lyrical language one might have recourse to Jean-Paul Sartre's discussion of the relationship between poetry and prose. Where the prose-writer is happy to use words as signs that indicate objects, the poet seizes on them as images or word-objects. Although we cannot accept Sartre's view that to the novelist words are transparent signs, we might follow him to the conclusion that 'the language of poetry rises up on the ruins of prose' (Jean-Paul Sartre, *Situations*, vol. 2 (Paris: Gallimard, 1948), p. 86). Unconvinced that he can 'make use of' words and that they are 'tame', the writer restores them to their 'wild' state in poetry. Aware that his primary language cannot explain the world, Meursault decides after all to strive after totality in this flood of images. Conversely, we might argue that, since the above-quoted passage depicts the world as a nightmare, Meursault defends himself against such terror by the wariness of his habitual language.

Traces of lyricism are found elsewhere in *The Stranger*. Part 1, Chapter 2, depicts the joy of a day at the beach with Marie: 'I had all the sky in my eyes and it was blue and golden' (34). Man and universe are fused, briefly and in ecstasy. More frequent are the passages where sounds and bodily sensations invade and capture the narrator's consciousness. After the decisive evening when he writes Raymond's letter, Meursault stands in the darkness: 'The building was calm and from the depths of the stairwell rose a dark, dank breath. I heard nothing but the throb of my blood which was booming in my ears' (55). In this we see a prophecy of the language of Chapter 6 where Meursault will kill the Arab.

Such moments are absent from Part 2, Chapters 1–4, which depict the imprisonment and trial, although they recur in the final chapter. Their absence from the bulk of Part 2 indicates the shift that has taken place in the novel. There the threat of death comes from the guillotine, whereas in Part 1 death is caught up with the mother and the Arab.

But the vagueness of the term 'caught up' reveals a difficulty in this argument. Sartre affirms that the structures of poetry and prose are quite different and between them 'there is nothing in common but the movement of the hand that traces the letters' (Sartre, *Situations*, vol. 2, p. 70). If one agrees with him, then it is unsatisfactory to designate the lyrical language of *The Stranger* as poetry. However, the problem exists in the text too: if the sun is convincing as a hostile force in the passage quoted, it seems to the present author virtually impossible to interpret it in the novel as a whole. We may and we will furnish explanations but we should not delude ourselves that they are altogether convincing. There are in Chapters 1 and 6 images of death that simply do not fit coherently into Meursault's narrative. We will return to the 'absence' or 'hollowness' which lies at the centre of *The Stranger*, but first we must describe more fully the primary language, the language of dissidence.

Camus's contemporaries, Sartre and Barthes, were struck by the non-literary appearance of *The Stranger*. Sentences are short and consist frequently of one main clause. Often the links among them are made by 'and' and 'but' or by a vague temporal conjunction like 'then' or 'after a while'. Some passages consist of enumeration, as when Meursault shows his irritation at being interrogated by listing his replies to the magistrate: 'Raymond, beach, swim, quarrel, beach again, the little spring, the sun and the five revolver shots' (105). Occasionally the time sequence is not merely vague but incorrect: on page 10 the reader cannot know precisely when Meursault went to Emmanuel's flat to collect the black armband.

The most obvious break with literary convention is the use — untranslatable into English — of the perfect instead of the past historic tense: 'I have done' instead of 'I did'. The past historic is the standard tense of the French novel while the perfect is usually the tense of conversation, so by choosing it Camus was refusing one of the principal signs by which a text declares that it belongs to literature.

Moreover, the past historic is the sign of a particular kind of narrative. It sets the action it depicts in a chronological sequence where other actions precede and follow. Although this is a temporal order, it can masquerade as a causality. So the past historic conveys to the reader the sense that the events narrated could not have unfolded in another manner, that their sequence possesses a certain legitimacy, and that behind the 'he' of the main character stands a divine narrator who comprehends the universe. Realist novelists of the nineteenth century, such as Balzac, use the past historic in this way which destroys, according to Barthes, 'the existential roots of experience' and constitutes 'a manifest lie' (Barthes, pp. 46, 50).

By contrast, the perfect is closer to the present and renders the action for itself. Each act becomes an event that is being lived rather than a segment of a greater whole. Indeed the concept of a whole is thus rendered problematic, because events occur rather than being created. To Barthes, Balzac's writing reflects and confirms the hegemony of the new capitalist middle class that was convinced of its power to shape history. Camus, along with other twentieth-century writers, is endeavouring to shake the ideological presuppositions upon which the traditional novel rests.

The perfect tense may lend to *The Stranger* an immediacy (although the problem of immediacy is complex), but it clearly lends an uncertainty which confirms the reader in his wariness. To complicate his task still further, the reader discovers that there are a number of past historic tenses in the novel. One of them occurs in a passage of Part 1, Chapter 1, where the language is growing more lyrical: 'La couleur rouge dans ce visage blafard me frappa' (26). But others occur in more characteristic passages, and there are also imperfect subjunctives − 'j'aurais préféré que maman ne mourût pas' (102) − although this tense too bears the sign of literature and is almost never used in conversation.

Literature is not easily escaped, and one doubts whether *The Stranger* is really seeking to escape it. Another trait of this novel is the string of deliberately banal adjectives like 'interesting, odd, natural, happy'. While they seem the stuff of everyday conversation, they are frequently deployed in sophisticated ways. In Part 1, Chapter 3, Meursault is declared by Marie to be 'odd' (70); three pages later he declares that a woman in the restaurant is 'odd'. It is left to the reader to decide who is odd and from which point of view oddness is to be judged, especially since Meursault elsewhere declares that he is 'exactly like everyone else' (103).

Similarly Meursault's lawyer asks him whether in not weeping over his mother he was overcoming his 'natural feelings' (102). This is ironic because society's concept of nature is so clearly false, but it is also enigmatic because the reader has not been allowed to know what Meursault's natural feelings are. To reinforce the irony, Meursault himself labels the legal process as 'natural' (110) several pages later.

Still more enigmatic is the adjective 'interesting'. Everything is interesting to Meursault because he refuses to make judgements about what is of greater or lesser importance. Yet even while perceiving the absence of judgement in Meursault's responses, the reader may decide that the word is justified. For example, the gruesome tale which the caretaker tells about burials in France and burials in Algeria is 'interesting' (16), because it underlines the difference between France and her colony which is a theme in the novel.

In these cases *The Stranger* culls literature from what seems 'a-literary' material. This is sometimes but not always true of Meursault's descriptions of people. In the closing pages of Part 1, Chapter 2, he sits on his balcony, looks down on the Sunday evening crowds and describes their appearance, gestures and movements. Of their inner life he tells us nothing, so we note merely the hair of a young girl, the red ties of the youths and the chants of soccer supporters.

Of course none of these details is in fact insignificant because in *The Stranger* Marie's long hair is a mark of female sexuality, the colour red is associated with aggression and male sexuality, while sport is linked with happiness. So each detail has its place in the larger structures of the novel. Yet they could be read as random physical details and − more importantly − Meursault invites us to do so when he mimics the gestures of the soccer supporters without knowing or caring which match they have seen.

Elsewhere, however, Meursault's descriptions are not those of a man-above-the-street. His language quickly becomes metaphorical and his judgements are evident in his depiction of the Parisian journalist who attends his trial: 'a small fellow who looked like a fattened up weasel with huge black-rimmed spectacles' (130). Even if the reader does not delve into the details − the colour black associated with Meursault's mother or the fact that Meursault cannot see the man's eyes − the pejorative nature of the simile is obvious.

When such passages are juxtaposed with the closing pages of Part 1, Chapter 2, we realize that Camus is constructing a language that affirms now its literary and now its a-literary identities. This language does not merely register the world like a passer-by nor does it organize the world like Balzac's. Aware that traditional literary discourse is a lie, it offers no new discourse. Hence the game of contradictions which is illustrated on the surface of the text by the proliferation of phrases like 'on the one hand, on the other'. Tormented by sexual fantasies in prison, Meursault notes: 'in one sense that disturbed me. But in another it killed time' (121). Writers judge, create hierarchies and proffer ideologies; Camus cannot stop himself doing it, but he can alert the reader that it is happening.

Often these expressions seem the signs of everyday language which does not seek to be precise: 'on thinking it over' and 'in a way' come into that category. But such expressions may be used in contexts that give them greater significance. Paraphrasing the lawyer for the prosecution, Meersault states that he had fired the last four bullets into the Arab 'after deliberation as it were' (153). Here the 'as it were' is Meursault's way of refuting the logic that the lawyer is ascribing to him.

Barthes concludes that *The Stranger* represents the 'zero degree' of writing; it is 'neutral and inert' because literature with its mythologies of omniscience and causality is banished. Camus's achievement is to free writing of these forms of servitude, so that it may directly confront the human condition. Then Barthes adds that such a zero degree is impossible and that out of the attempt to create it 'writing is reborn' (Barthes, pp. 110–11). The last comment seems to the present author important because *The Stranger* does not really banish the signs of literature but rather it presents them as forms of authority and order. It reminds us that a banal adjective like 'natural' contains judgements by leaving the reader stranded among several possible judgements. So the term 'neutral' does not seem appropriate, and we would prefer to restate our view that *The Stranger* is above all a self-aware text, as a glance at its narrative form reveals.

To many contemporary critics narrators, like characters and authors, are of little interest because they are personifications: rhetorical figures that the reader may invent but that are unreal alongside the reality of the written page. As we have seen, *The Stranger* is a novel that might encourage such a view because Camus has tried to abolish the traditional author. Although one may decide that he treats his narrator with similar lack of ceremony, it is useful for that very reason to consider the question.

One might begin with the topic of the constraints of literature. *The Stranger* was a text to be published by the house of Gallimard, which had a proven interest in avant-garde writing, but which offered its readers a series of familiar products. So *The Stranger* had to fit the category called 'the novel'. Of the many kinds of novels, Camus chose the 'I' form and the journal. But, if it was obvious that he would not choose the omniscient author, the 'he' of a hero and the sprawl of characters, that did not in itself free him of constraints.

The journal is a form where an 'I', who is both character and narrator, filters events through an awareness. A recognized genre of French writing, it was favoured by Gide and other *NRF* writers because it gives priority to the inner life. The reader becomes a confidant who is seduced into believing what the 'I' reveals, while the character usually develops throughout the book; by the time he becomes a narrator at the end, he can look back and trace his evolution. So there is a series of presuppositions: that the inner life is important and can be discussed with someone else, and that it is coherent. Camus's innovation is to criticize this form by using it for a character-narrator who partially rejects those presuppositions. This enables him to demonstrate once more that the supposed harmony of the work of art is an illusion.

One might argue crudely that Meursault would be most unlikely to keep a journal. Shunning introspection and trusting only the realities of the senses, he would surely not commit his thoughts to paper. He tells his lawyer in Part 2, Chapter 1, that 'I had rather lost the habit of questioning myself' (102). When we examine the chronological sequence, we shall see that Part 1, Chapter 1, is supposedly written on Friday evening after he returns from the funeral; yet it is obvious that he is too exhausted to write anything. While such objections are crude because they presuppose a concept of realism that *The Stranger* rejects, it remains true that Camus has selected the literary form that requires the highest degree of awareness and has inserted into it a narrator whose very identity consists in the inadequacy of his awareness.

Or rather, the problem changes as the novel goes on. A glance at the temporal indications which the text contains and which have been examined by Barrier, Fitch and others reveals this. *The Stranger* appears to be a journal written at different moments and in several chunks. The first section is made up of the initial two paragraphs because Meursault uses the future tense — 'I shall get the two o'clock bus' (9). The rest of the chapter would constitute the second section which was written on Friday evening. Chapter 2 announces by its use of 'yesterday' and 'today' that it is being started on Saturday, although a reference to 'the evening' rather than 'this evening' (35) would imply that it was composed on Sunday. The flaw in the chronology hints that Camus does not wish to present a temporal structure that is clear.

The fourth chunk is made up of Chapter 3, which is written on Monday evening, as the 'today' (43) proclaims. Then Chapter 4 would constitute the fifth section written on the following Sunday, since Meursault 'has worked well all week' (57) and since 'yesterday' is Saturday (57). Yet there is a flaw here too, because at the end of the chapter Meursault uses not 'tomorrow' but 'the next day' (66), which implies that the chapter was written later.

The rest of the book contains no temporal indicators that would prevent us from believing that it was written after the trial and at some point during the events of the last chapter. This segment is closer to the orthodox journal-novel because, as we shall see, Meursault grows in awareness in Part 2. Not only would his approaching death offer him a plausible pretext for writing, but he has undergone an evolution which he is able to trace.

There remains the problem of Part 1, Chapter 5, whose last paragraph marks the beginning of such awareness — 'I understood that I had destroyed the balance of the day' (95). But the lyrical language which depicts the murder of the Arab does not fit with the language prevailing in either Part 1 or Part 2, while the early pages of this chapter grow naturally out of Part 1, Chapter 4. One might conclude that there are two narrative time-structures: the second is the orthodox reconstruction of the journal-novel, while the first seeks specifically to avoid coherence.

The possible relationship between the two halves of the

novel will be discussed shortly, but we may note here that *The Stranger* draws attention to the artifice of its form in other ways. In Part 1, Chapter 1, Meursault writes of the pensioners: 'I had the impression that the dead woman lying in their midst meant nothing in their eyes. Now I think my impression was false' (21). When is this 'now'? If Meursault is speaking directly after the funeral, one can only respond that he nowhere else displays such awareness. Could it be the Meursault who is waiting to be guillotined? He does possess the awareness, but it would imply that he has written the entire book and that the 'tomorrows' are inserted to mislead. The most likely answer is that Camus is drawing attention to Meursault's twin roles as mourner and narrator, and hinting that they do not necessarily fit together.

Nor is the doubt limited to the temporal structure. When the warden tells him that his mother has asked for a religious funeral, Meursault notes: 'Although she was not an atheist, mother had never in her life thought about religion' (13). This is puzzling since Meursault elsewhere professes to know nothing of other people's feelings and little of his own. If he here slips into the role of the omniscient author, it is surely a provocation that Camus has inserted to draw attention to that agnosticism. A trace of agnosticism recurs in the sentence that begins Part 2, Chapter 2: 'There are things I have never liked talking about' (113). Although these 'things' are eventually identified as 'the hour without a name', namely, the prison evenings, the word 'never' casts a restrospective doubt over the preceding chapters.

The issue of when and how *The Stranger* is being narrated leads to the question of what one is supposed to feel towards Meursault. As a narrator he is an agnostic and as a character he is indifferent. The concept of indifference will be discussed several times in this study, but here we would like to suggest that it leads to further hesitation on the reader's part and that this too is a criticism of the traditional novel, where the reader is led to 'identify' with the hero.

A famous example of indifference is Meursault's response

when Marie asks whether he loves her: 'I replied that that didn't mean anything, but that I thought I did not' (59). The reply is intriguing (Meursault might say it is 'interesting') because it takes Marie's question and reformulates it in a more abstract manner; the first part of Meursault's answer is that the entity of love either does not exist or cannot be embraced by language. This in turn leads back to Meursault the narrator, who is unable to tell us anything about emotions. The second half may be interpreted in two different ways: as a protest against Marie's idealization and as an inability to feel. Each explanation possesses a certain validity. By confusing sexual desire and love Marie is indulging in a false romanticism, which blinds her to her body and her situation as a working-class woman. Conversely, Meursault reveals that he is incapable of opening to a woman. The reader, who is probably more tempted by the second interpretation, should not discount either, because the life Meursault leads contains both ingredients: honesty as well as sterility, protest as well as alienation.

The theme to be stressed here is that the reader is unable to decide which of the two is more important and whether any combination of the two might be considered a full explanation. He is thus unable to understand the character Meursault and to feel for him the imaginative sympathy that he feels for a traditional hero. Indeed the use of the term 'hero' is inappropriate.

Other such examples abound in the first half of *The Stranger*. When Marie asks Meursault to marry her, his reply seems to emphasize protest rather than alienation. Having declared that 'it was all the same to me' (69), he specifically denies that marriage is a serious matter. But here again his inability to feel is present in his willingness to marry or not to marry a woman to whom marriage is important. A far greater alienation is present in his refusal to intervene when Raymond beats up the Arab woman. Told by Marie that the woman's cries are 'terrible', Meursault 'did not reply' (60).

One does not wish to imply that there are no reasons for Meursault's behaviour. It will be argued later that there are two kinds of reasons — psychoanalytical and political — but neither renders Meursault a comprehensible, much less a sympathetic, character. The absence of direct explanations in the narration erects a barrier between Meursault and the reader, who had expected to be a confidant but finds himself a stranger.

This is, in Sartre's words, a novel 'that does not explain' (Sartre, 'Explication de *L'Etranger*', p. 105). One might go further and say that it *ostentatiously* does not explain, because the theme of comprehension is stressed. There are three moments of privileged awareness in Part 1, Chapters 1 and 6, and in Part 2, Chapter 5. All will be discussed later, but here one may mention that they are linked with the experience of death and wrapped in the second, lyrical language (albeit not completely). At the opposite pole stands the frequent satire of comprehension. When Raymond tells Meursault that 'among men you could always understand one another' (55), the remark is ironic because it is the postscript to the puzzling episode where Meursault writes the letter to the Arab woman. When the head warden of the prison congratulates Meursault on his ability to understand the penal system — 'you understand things, you do' (121), the reader is tempted to laugh.

Most examples in the first half of the novel come between the two extremes. On at least two occasions Meursault furnishes explanations: he interprets a film for Emmanuel, and he informs Salamano how stray dogs are dealt with by the city of Algiers. This marks Meursault as a man who has greater awareness than his working-class friends, and yet in the second case he does not know all the details.

It is not, then, that life is a puzzle before which Meursault throws up his hands and invites the reader to do the same. That would be reassuring and simple. Certainly Meursault's use of the adjective 'interesting' implies that he does not wish to make judgements, but even his most agnostic comments contain some. When he hears Salamano beating his dog he notes: 'Céleste always says, "It's unfortunate", but really no one can know' (46). At first his incomprehension appears as a kind of intellectual indifference but, as always, indifference is a complex concept. Meursault's remark may be read as a rebuke to Céleste's working-class sentimentality and even as a correct insight. For the reader subsequently learns that the relationship between Salamano and his dog contains a kind of love and is not simple brutality.

It appears to me that the language and narrative structure of *The Stranger* lead us to two conclusions. The first is that, as in his theatre experiments, Camus is affirming that art is no different from the rest of the universe and should not pretend to a harmony or a perfection which it cannot possess. In a review of Sartre's *Nausea*, Camus criticizes the hope of salvation by literature. It is 'derisory', he states, to believe that writing can provide answers ('*La Nausée* de J.-P. Sartre', *OC* 2,1419). By satirizing the language of authority in *The Stranger* he is demonstrating that such answers are disguised forms of tyranny.

However, the difference in narrative structure between the first and second halves of the novel declares that they should not be read in the same manner. As Fitch has pointed out, the trial chapters contain interpretations of the first half of the book. Undertaken chiefly by the two lawyers, these exegeses are so obviously wrong as to invite the reader to doubt his own interpretations. Despite this, Part 2 does allow itself to be explained and, we shall argue, Meursault becomes less and less of a stranger, until at the end the reader can identify with him. Moreover, by now Meursault has come to understand his own existence. Whether this explanation allows the reader retrospectively to interpret Part 1 is a separate issue and it is my opinion that it does not. The two parts do not fit neatly together, and the more disturbing features of Part 1 must be forgotten before the reader's sympathy and understanding may be won. The language of dissidence must, for example, become less an interrogation of itself and more an irony that mocks the judges.

The second and more difficult conclusion is that in Part 1 Meersault's awareness is not, as Sartre maintained, 'a pure passivity' (Sartre, 'Explication de *L'Etranger*', p. 115). Not merely is his agnosticism a form of protest, it is — even in its futility — the mark of his existence as an individual. While the second, lyrical language is a form of terror that lurks in the background of his life, the narrator can ward it off by ambiguity just as the character Meursault keeps it at bay with indifference. We must now consider the first emissary of death, the mother.

A mother unmourned?

Of Meursault's life with his mother we learn slightly more than we might imagine. In Part 1, Chapter 1, he notes that 'when she was at home mother spent her time watching me in silence' (12). The 'look' is a complex motif in *The Stranger*, where it indicates the lack of closer forms of contact. Or at least this is true of Meursault's glances at people unless he manages to see their eyes, in which case he becomes conscious of an awareness. Usually he does not, and he is left to puzzle over a possibly hostile otherness. Here it appears that he has inherited his look from his mother.

Silence is another attribute they share and it is, as we have already said, a mark both of integrity and of alienation. One might conclude that the mother is an intense, troubling presence in his existence, and that he might respond intensely to her. After her departure from their flat he continues to live with her in the sense that he brings her furniture into his bedroom and makes no use of the other rooms. A close and — so the psychoanalytical reading would run — incestuous bond unites them. Even the mirror in which he looks at himself is hers — 'the yellowing glass of the wardrobe' (36).

Is it too rash to suggest, then, that Meursault's indifference at her funeral is not a conventional indifference but the mark of a deeper relationship which contains love and hatred, neither of which can be expressed? His lack of feeling is both an attempt to rid himself of her and the sign of his identification with her. As Jean Gassin puts it, Meursault's indifference 'towards his mother is merely a way of turning against her the mortal indifference that emanates from her' (Gassin,

p. 214). His is an attitude of frozen defiance in the face of a mother whose death, like her life, menaces his identity and prevents him from going through a genuine mourning, that would liberate him from her.

Signs of guilt find their way into the text. When asking his boss for time off he adds: 'It's not my fault' (9); at the home he feels that the warden is criticizing him for placing his mother there: 'I thought he was reproaching me with something' (11); with Marie he notes: 'Anyway, you are always a bit at fault' (35). Yet this guilt remains unfocused and in the case of the warden he is not really being reproached with anything. So the reader is left unable to decide what the precise nature of the guilt might be.

Examples of his indifference towards his mother's death abound: not opening the coffin to look at her, not weeping, not remaining after the funeral to meditate at her grave, not knowing how old she was, drinking coffee with milk and smoking during the wake, and the next day going to the cinema and beginning a sexual relationship with Marie. Moreover, the narrator offers no evidence of grief, leaving the reader with the sense that this might, after all, be conventional indifference.

There is, however, evidence to indicate that it is not, that Meursault is engaged in an unwitting protest against society's desire to conjure death away, and that indifference is a way to survive a shattering experience. It might be worthwhile reiterating that the object of this analysis is not to demonstrate that Meursault is in reality a loving son (a fiction that will be expounded by the defence lawyer), but rather that he is haunted by death and unable to come to grips with grief and love.

The issue of his mother's age is a conflict between Meursault's sense of time as lived – the 'yesterdays' and 'todays' – and society's view that time may be measured abstractly. On the question of opening the coffin, we remember that Meursault does wish to see his mother when he arrives at the home; it is only after encountering, via the warden and the caretaker, society's view of death that he changes his mind. Another reason is that – so we shall argue – he grows progressively less able to face death as the chapter goes on.

The cigarette is interesting because Meursault asks himself the question: 'I wanted to smoke then. But I hesitated because I didn't know whether I could in front of mother. I thought about it: it had no importance' (17). Meursault's agnosticism comes into play: in the face of a coffin, the decision whether or not to smoke has no significance. This is a more troubling view of death than the warden's.

The clearest case where seeming casualness masks distress is when Meursault does not linger near the grave. By the end of the chapter he has undergone the sun's onslaught and must at all costs escape. His departure from the cemetery is presented as a flight – he speaks of 'my joy when the bus got to the nest of lights of Algiers' (31) – and marks relief rather than carelessness. A brief analysis of the funeral will reinforce this conclusion.

The sequence of events runs from Meursault's initial desire to look at his mother, through the ideology of society represented by the warden, and on to the meetings with the caretaker and the Arab nurse. Then the hallucination builds up as the mother's friends arrive, there is a second meeting with the warden and a moment of insight as the funeral procession begins. From then on the hallucination grows as the sun becomes more hostile and compels Meursault to flee.

As soon as he arrives, Meursault is diverted by the warden towards the gestures of inauthentic mourning. The warden seeks to absolve Meursault of the guilt he may have incurred by placing his mother in the home: 'she had friends, people of her own age' (11). In reply Meursault does not disagree but, when he talks of his mother's life in the home, he attributes her behaviour to habit. Soon he ceases to listen to the warden.

In the morgue he meets the caretaker and the Arab nurse, whose place in the social structure of *The Stranger* will be discussed later, and then groups of his mother's friends. By now the language of the chapter is changing and there is an emphasis on the colour white – 'it was a bright, whitewashed room' (13). Throughout the next pages white will be associated with black — and occasionally with red — as a colour that threatens Meursault. If white is traditionally linked with knowledge, then it is here the knowledge of death which humans cannot face. The brightness of white is transmitted by other objects, notably the screws of the coffin which stand out against the wood; it is after noting these screws that Meursault refuses to have the coffin opened. The white light grows steadily more hostile — Mersault is 'blinded' and 'worried' (17) by it — and it is outside his control for it cannot be dimmed.

When the morgue is 'even more dazzlingly white' (18), the pensioners enter and Meursault, as ever, observes concrete details: the aprons of the women and the walking sticks of the men. But this is an occasion when physical signs, unaccompanied by emotional sympathy (for Meursault dislikes the lament of a woman who proclaims herself his mother's friend), take on an imaginative meaning. Unable to see the men's eyes, he also cannot interpret their nods, but he concludes the paragraph by stating: 'For a moment I had the ridiculous impression that they were there to judge me' (19). Guilt, distrust of others and a premonition of his trial are lurking behind his lack of obvious emotion.

During his second encounter with the warden Meursault has to sign documents, thus affirming by the act of writing that his mother is dead. Then the warden is joined by the other representative of authority, the priest, who addresses Meursault as 'my son' (25), the warden having previously called him 'my dear child' (11). However, the role of society in this scene is slight, for the major protagonist now enters: the sun.

'The sky was already full of sunshine. It started to weigh down on the earth and the heat increased rapidly' (26). The sun takes over the role played by the white light, and at the same time — to heighten the non-realistic tone — the dominant colour shifts from white to black. What then does the sun represent?

This question will be posed again in our discussion of Part

1, Chapter 6, and the answer will be different, but in either chapter it seems difficult to argue that the sun represents some natural order. Certainly Meursault often tries to identify with nature and even here he contrasts the countryside with mornings in Algiers when he leaves for his office. The antithesis of country–town and the rejection of the values of work are obvious. Yet in this chapter nature is equally alien to man and far more powerful. There is in *The Stranger* no consistent view of the sun and, while it is part of a specifically Algerian brand of nature that will be discussed in connection with Chapter 6, it seems necessary to resort to other interpretations of Chapter 1.

A psychoanalytical reading might identify the sea with the mother and the sun with the father. So the sun is the agent of a father determined to punish his son for his incestuous relationship with his mother. But, as Gassin points out, Camus does not make such a simple distinction. Here, as in Chapter 6, the sun and the sea act together — the sea is present at the funeral as 'the smell of salt' (22), which the winds carry over the mountains from the coast — and are associated with the mother. So the sun is, to borrow another of Gassin's phrases, an agent of 'the evil Mother' who is punishing her son for his inability to love her (Gassin, p. 226).

Certainly the sun dominates the procession: 'the blazing sun, which caused the countryside to shimmer, made it inhuman and depressing' (27). Two pages later comes the passage already quoted, where the sun's aggression is linked to black, the mother's colour.

However, Meursault enjoys a moment of insight which is significantly situated after the first sally of the sun but before the heat becomes unbearable. It is thus shaped by contact with death, but also by resistance to it. When the warden tells Meursault that his mother and Pérez used to walk to the village each evening, Meursault broods: 'Through the lines of cypress trees that led to the hills up near the sky, this reddish, green land, these scattered houses with their clear outlines, I understood mother. In this region evening must be a melancholic truce' (27). This insight will be elaborated on the closing pages of the book, but already its significance is apparent. The associations of countryside, of the colours green (a happy colour to Camus) and a gentler red, and of the evening when the sun is less strong, enable Meursault to perceive his mother as a person separate from him. With Pérez, who plays the role of her husband without being Meursault's father, she leads an existence free from the oedipal struggle. However, this moment of maturity, when Meursault is reconciled with her and is able − if the adjective 'melancholic' is any guide − to mourn her, vanishes and the sun returns.

Pérez is an important figure in the funeral for, if he is close to Meursault but not in authority over him, he may be perceived as acting out a grief that Meursault is unable to express. At the trial Pérez's evidence is, unlike the evidence of the warden and the caretaker, not damaging to his adopted son.

Pérez's portrait is another case where the narration offers physical details that cannot avoid, try as they might, possessing non-physical significance. First, since his tie does not fit he does not belong among the normal mourners, like the warden. Secondly, with his white hair, black tie and red ears he sums up in a comical manner the key colours of the chapter. While mocking him, Meursault hints that he is a serious person; Pérez is both 'curious' (26) and 'dignified' (28) and, as if to underline his special role, he keeps leaving and rejoining the procession. In Meursault's final hallucination Pérez appears in his two different guises, which are complementary opposites because they are equally distant from Meursault's apparent calm. When he finally faints, Pérez is an object − he looked like 'a broken doll' (31) − but a moment earlier he had stood 'with huge tears of exhaustion and distress' (30).

By now the narration retains only faint traces of its self-awareness. The sense impressions, ever more discordant, convey further images of aggression: the red of the sun reappears in the geraniums of the cemetery and the earth, while the colour white returns in the roots of the plants that have been torn up. Seizing on a remark by the chief nurse that proclaims its triviality. Meursault launches the prophetic utterance that 'there was no way out' (30); this too looks forward to the trial and will turn up in the closing pages. Both as character and as narrator, Meursault is falling apart like Pérez, and only flight can save him. The last sentence of the chapter takes up twelve lines, most of them short, parallel clauses that the narrator cannot organize.

Of this chapter Gassin writes: 'The killing of the Arab is the second murder committed by Meursault. The first had been the murder of his own mother disguised as a burial' (Gassin, p. 27). There is every justification for such a Freudian reading since, not merely can Meursault's indifference be read as hatred of a mother who continues to obsess him, but the traces of guilt would lead us to see in her death a wish-fulfilment. This does not, of course, prevent Meursault from feeling an unavowed love for his mother, which helps increase the guilt and explains the obsession.

We would like further to stress that the aspect of the oedipal struggle depicted by *The Stranger* is the threat to the son. Unable to separate his own identity from his mother's, Meursault is brought close to death and can escape only by hastily laying her in her grave. So she may be said to die in his stead. We must also admit that this is not a complete inter-pretation of a difficult chapter. It is not merely that by its calculated ambiguity *The Stranger* leaves open the possibility that Meursault's indifference is sheer carelessness, but that the relationship between mother and the sun is not rendered explicit by the text. The sun remains an image and eludes close definition.

However, the view that the mother's death is crucial to Meursault receives support from the next four chapters. Although the subplots they depict seem to unfold at random, the friendships Meursault strikes up with Salamano and Ray-mond and the relationship he begins with Marie are re-enactments of his dealings with his mother.

This is most obvious in the case of Marie Cardonna, who appears to represent a solution to the mother's death: Meur-sault will now direct his energies towards another woman.

Instead he refuses to love her, making the comment that has already been quoted. This refusal is in part an assertion of other, more concrete, values, namely, the values of the body that are exemplified in the early pages of Chapter 2: sport, physical beauty and sexual pleasure.

In this context, Camus's treatment of women is interesting because Marie is not seduced by Meursault, but is an equal partner. She was formerly 'a typist in my office and at the time I wanted her. She wanted me too, I believe' (34). After their first night together she gets up and leaves before he awakens. Only when she seeks love and marriage, the traditional values of women, will Meursault rebuff her.

In Chapter 2 colours change and the key colour becomes brown, the hue of Marie's sun-tanned body. The link between man and nature is restored, for the sun and the sea preside over their meeting. There is even the note of lyricism to hint that man might indeed be part of a harmonious nature.

Sexuality, grace and athleticism are values that are developed in Camus's other books. If the bond with the mother was love, then love is a kind of death and life is to be found in the body. However, we must repeat that there is alienation in Meursault's view, in that he is unable to imagine any kind of love other than the love-death he has known with his mother. So even as he flees her she retains her power over him.

In the episode of Salamano many observers have recognized parallels between Salamano and his dog and Meursault and his mother. Salamano has lived a life of alienation working on the railway whereas he had wished to be an actor, and he was married to a woman with whom he was not happy but to whom he grew accustomed. Habit, perceived both as resignation and stoicism, is another theme which Meursault has inherited from his mother: 'Mother had the idea and she repeated it often, that you eventually got used to anything' (120). The dog, which Salamano obtained after his wife's death, replaces her and the child they never had: 'He had had to feed it with a bottle. But, since a dog doesn't live as long as a man, they had grown old together' (74).

The link between the dog and Meursault's mother is explicit — Salamano 'told me that mother liked his dog very much' (75) — and the dog disappears the week after her death. Salamano's open expression of his grief must then be an indication of Meursault's repressed feelings. On hearing him weep Meursault notes: 'I thought of mother, I don't know why' (65).

The darker side of Salamano's dealings with the dog offers further parallels with Meursault and his mother. Perhaps Meursault's indifference to the way Salamano beats his pet is not merely an inability to feel repugnance for sadism, but an approval which reflects his feelings of hostility towards his mother. If so, then there is a progression from the denial of love for Marie to the cruelty in which he participates towards the dog. This view is confirmed when further comparisons are drawn with the relationship of Raymond Sintès and the Arab woman.

The friendship between Raymond and Meursault revolves around displays of masculinity and hostility towards women (and towards Arabs, as will be discussed later). Raymond's room, the setting for the friendship, is replete with photos of boxers and nudes and he begins by describing to Meursault how he beat up the woman and then her brother in a dispute about virility. Further accoutrements of masculinity abound: drinking, smoking, billiards and a proposed visit to a brothel. The friendship is itself a sign of masculinity: Raymond keeps describing Meursault as a 'pal' (54).

This is the episode where, as already discussed, Meursault's indifference contains the fewest elements of protest and the highest degree of alienation. By writing the letter, Meursault is participating in Raymond's brutality towards women, and he himself invites us to draw the parallels not merely with Chapter 6 but retrospectively with Chapter 1. When leaving Raymond's flat he utters the phrase: 'I heard nothing but the throb of my blood which was booming in my ears' (55); this harks back to the sentence 'I could feel my blood beating in my temples' (30), which he notes during the funeral. At this same moment the dog 'moaned in old Salamano's room' (56).

So the text invites the reader to see both the Raymond and Salamano episodes as forms of sadism directed against the mother.

Behind the seemingly random tales that are told in the first half of *The Stranger* there lies a logic. Far from being blithely indifferent, Meursault is still struggling against his mother. Hidden away in *The Stranger* lies a psychoanalytical novel, where the mother, although dead, continues to strike at her son who strikes back. However, with the introduction of Raymond's Arab mistress a direct link has been established between the mother and the Arab, and the reader is aware that there is also a political novel in *The Stranger*.

Class and race

Many critics would agree that a novel, since it must appear probable to its readers, will mirror the social structures of the outside world with certain deformations and criticisms. Critics who dislike the notion of probability will still accept that language shapes and is shaped by the surrounding society. Either way *The Stranger* merits a political analysis, because it portrays the various groups of French-Algeria and because its various languages bear the marks of social conflict.

Such an analysis begins with the key and contradictory role of the French-Algerian working class. *The Stranger* depicts a tension between the ruling and the working class or between the language of authority and either the stumbling speech of Céleste or Meursault's language of dissent. But there is also a conflict between all those who use the French language — the Europeans — and those forced into silence — the Arabs. The two tensions overlap but not easily, which explains the impossible position of the French-Algerian working class, caught as it is between a ruling class which tends to identify with mainland France, and the indigenous, Arab population. In its depiction of this contradiction *The Stranger* is less the expression of a colonial society than an insight into it.

In the first half of the book the representatives of power are the warden of the home and the boss, both of whom are un-named and are known to the reader only by their function. The former represents the softer aspect of authority: pater-nalistic control over the pensioners, to whom the warden awards or refuses permission to attend different parts of the funeral; concern to banish death by an elaborate social ritual; and alliance with the priest who represents orthodox Catholicism. The warden's task is to run the institution smoothly — to avoid 'making our work difficult' (12) — and the pensioners have been defined by the state as people who no longer have the freedom to make their own decisions.

The boss expresses the values of liberal capitalism: work, commerce, ambition and freedom to rise in society as long as one adheres to its credo. Thus he doesn't 'seem pleased' when Meursault asks for time off to attend the funeral. The next Monday he asks Meursault how old his mother was, turning her death into a matter of statistics. Meursault gives him a figure, and 'I don't known why, but he seemed relieved and he appeared to consider that the matter was closed' (43). Here again Meursault's 'I don't know why' underlines his dissent from the boss's values.

The clash is more open in Chapter 5, where the boss offers Meursault promotion and a job in Paris. First the offer is made as 'a change of life' — the vocabulary of humanism — and then as a matter of ambition, the lack of which is 'disastrous in business' (69) — the vocabulary of economics. Meursault's reply shows no trace of his usual agnosticism: 'I answered that you never changed your life, that anyway one life was as good as another and mine seemed all right to me' (69). In this are traces of the existentialist view that life is to be lived not judged or compared; but there is also the working-class sense that concepts of ambition and career are fictions and that work is an unpleasant necessity to which one submits. Either way, the middle-class notions that work can be rewarding and that a career leads one to some chosen goal are rejected.

Meursault, uncharacteristically, offers further explana-tions: 'When I was a student I had lots of ambitions of this kind. But when I had to stop studying I quickly realized that it was all unimportant' (69). Why did he have to stop? For lack of money? If so, we might see in him a familiar French figure: the boy of working-class background who rises via the education system and then, perceiving the unfairness of society, turns away from it. Here again the text does not provide us with enough information to draw such conclusions. Yet Meursault's sense of alienation from the boss's values pervades the book and seems to me all the more convincing because it finds no political outlet.

One reason may be that Meursault is a white-collar worker who makes his living by writing. A desk, a pen and bills of lading are the instruments of his employment. This not only leaves him exposed to the boss's ideology, but separates him from the comradeship of manual workers and their political expressions, such as trade unions. Of his circle of friends, Emmanuel is employed sending out the parcels and hence is a step further away from writing, while Marie exemplifies white-collar alienation because, as a secretary, she earns her living by transcribing words that belong not to her but to people who are in authority over her. Significantly, the only time she speaks of her work is in Part 2, when she visits Meursault in prison.

If she is a prisoner of the language of authority, then Céleste's fate is to strive for authenticity by using words that stifle it. His remark to Meursault, 'You only have one mother' (10), is an attempt to express sympathy that is distorted into a propositional statement. Comic and yet moving, his halting speech contrasts with Raymond's fluency, and this opposition sums up the contradictory position of the French-Algerian working class.

The language of the body is linked with this class: with Marie most obviously, and also with Emmanuel, who likes to run. Conversely, the boss, who considers that the sensation of drying oneself on a soggy roller-towel is unpleasant but 'without importance' (44), has no sense of his body because he is lost in a world of abstractions and objects. So *The Stranger* asserts not merely that the body has its language, but that the decision to ignore that language is part of the alienation of capitalism. However, here again Raymond is different, for he does not swim with Meursault and Marie and, where Marie's body is sun-tanned, his arms are 'very white beneath the black hairs' (78), which disgusts Meursault.

Although Meursault's friendship with Raymond has been interpreted as a display of masculinity which is an act of defiance against his mother, it also contains class elements. The two share a dislike for the representatives of authority, as is demonstrated when Raymond beats up the Arab woman and Meursault – unlike Marie – refuses to call a policeman: 'I told her that I didn't like policemen' (60). This leads him to move away from the employed, respectable working class towards the underworld with which Raymond flaunts his allegiance.

One reason may be that Meursault is not an integral part of that class, since in his neighbourhood he is criticized for placing his mother in the home. His response, however, cuts through platitudes about love: 'For a long time she had had nothing to say to me and she was bored on her own' (75). In its context Meursault's remark contains an element of protest, directed against the working class which has interiorized the false humanism of its masters. The attitude of the neighbourhood anticipates the speeches that the prosecuting lawyer will make at the trial.

Elsewhere Meursault plays the same role: he implicitly rebukes Céleste for his sentimental attitude towards Salamano's dog and he corrects Marie's view of marriage: 'She said to me that marriage is a serious matter. I replied: "No"' (69). The direct speech reinforces Meursault's rejection of a social and religious institution. Without drawing any coherent political conclusions, he embodies, through his indifference, his refusal of the way that working-class people seek to hide from themselves the alienation in which they live. This is why he feels a bond with his friends and yet criticizes their weakness. His is a more radical attitude, which will find expression in Part 2, where he will impose his irony on the lawyers' rhetoric.

The friendship with Raymond, who is probably a pimp masquerading as a warehouse worker and who is himself disliked in the neighbourhood, is then a gesture of opposition. It is also a gesture of solidarity with a man of unrelenting hostility towards Arabs.

For, if the class lines are clearly drawn, the colonial situation complicates them. At each critical moment of Part 1 the three groups are present: before Meursault's mother's coffin stand the Parisian caretaker, the pied-noir Meursault and the Arab nurse; on the beach in Chapter 6 are Masson's Parisian wife, Meursault and the Arab brother. Significantly, when Meursault is condemned to death in Part 2 there are no Arabs present, although the Parisian journalist is there.

Throughout the novel metropolitan France is depicted as separate from Algeria, and is portrayed unfavourably. The warden is linked to France because he wears the Legion of Honour, while the Parisian caretaker is an usurper who, having entered the home as an indigent, obtained a post which gives him an authority over the other old people. In making the distinction between French and Algerian funerals he insists on the role of the heat, thus bringing out the sun as a cultural and political rather than natural or psychoanalytical entity.

Meursault questions the caretaker's authority, but his dislike of France emerges more clearly in the episode where his boss wants to send him to Paris. Its role as the centre of commerce makes it a citadel of oppression of the pied-noir working class, and later Meursault elaborates on his dislike in a conversation with Marie, which once more pits submission against a more radical discourse. Whereas she has the provincial's admiration for the capital, he asserts: 'It's dirty. There are pigeons and black courtyards. The people have white skins' (70). The two colours associated with the mother are attributed to the mother-country, while the importance of Marie's brown skin is made clearer: it defines her as a pied-noir.

Distrustful of France, the pied-noir finds his dealings with Arabs no easier. It is here that *The Stranger* passes from a discourse that is psychoanalytical — the identification of the Arab with the mother — to a discourse that is political — the Arab as brother, rival and enemy.

In the morgue of Chapter 1 (as if foreshadowing Chapter 6) stands the nurse: 'Near the bier there was also an Arab nurse' (14). The colour scheme is striking because three times the Arab will be associated with blue — the Arab men wear blue dungarees — and in another work, *The Exile and the Kingdom*, Camus repeats the association, this time linking the Arab with the blue sky. But if the Arab appears to belong to the world of nature, that is, Camus knows, a European's false perception. For the Arab is living in a colonial society and the nurse wears a uniform that indicates her social function. Her task is to watch over the French-Algerian dead in a home where no Arabs are present. This prepares us for the worse plight of the other Arabs who are driven into prostitution, idleness and prison.

Meursault tries twice to look at the nurse, but neither time is he able to detect her eyes. So even the flawed and often hostile contact, that stems from encountering another awareness, is lacking. The second time he interprets her behaviour from her gestures: 'judging from the movement of her arm I thought she was knitting' (18). The first time he can see 'nothing of her face except the whiteness of a bandage' (15). In *Betwixt and Between* knitting is associated with the mother (who is knitting an outfit of black and white), and the presence of the colour white here strengthens the nurse's role as surrogate mother.

A further detail is the tumour which has eaten away her nose. The illness, which will presumably kill her, makes her even more like the mother, but it also represents an impersonal act of brutality. As such it stands outside of history, and yet it foreshadows the brutalities that stem not from fate but from the colonial system. So, although the nurse, who comes and goes without regard to Meursault or the caretaker, vanishes from the novel, she has established the Arab as a disturbing presence and her whiteness may be said to trigger the intense white light which so troubles Meursault.

In not speaking she offers parallels with the mother and with Meursault. We will return to this matter, but here we may note that the silence is a sign both of oppression and of authenticity. The next Arab, Raymond's mistress, will utter the cry when Raymond beats her for the second time and will then add a brief sentence that unmasks him: 'He has beaten me up. He's a pimp' (61). This — the language of denunciation — cuts through Raymond's lies and may be read as an outburst of revolt against the two occasions when he imposes his language on her and her brother, by describing to Meursault how he beat them up.

If this woman too is a surrogate of the mother, the discourse on Arabs has nonetheless shifted because the brutality done to her is committed by a French-Algerian. It appears that from this point on psychoanalytical interpretations do not in themselves suffice. For, while such readings reaffirm that the Arab on the beach is an agent of the mother, they do not answer the questions of why the agent is an Arab. One might speculate that, as the original inhabitant of North Africa, the Arab is identified with the mother or the father, just as the mother is briefly linked with metropolitan France, that other threat to the pied-noir.

But this is a nebulous argument and we must attempt a political reading that will trace the growing rivalry between the French-Algerians, Raymond and Meursault, and the Arabs. We cannot then agree with Jean Gassin who asserts that the origins of Meursault's 'strangeness' are psychoanalytical but not political (Gassin p. 88). Why should they not be both? Meursault's sense that his identity is being menaced by his mother overlaps with his sense that his identity as a pied-noir is being menaced by the Arab. The psychoanalytical gives way to the political in the movement from Part 1, Chapter 1, to Part 1, Chapter 6. That Meursault does not feel hostility to Arabs, or, more correctly, that Meursault, the narrator, does not articulate hostility, is not an objection when we remember all the other things he does not tell us. Indeed in this case his silence is the sign within the text of the official French-Algerian ideology of assimilation.

In Raymond's dealings with the Arab woman and her brother there is a political dimension that is linked with the issue of manhood. The position of woman in a colonial society has been analysed often: she is a prize for colonizer and colonized to fight over. So here the Arab woman is reduced by the European, Raymond, to a prostitute, while her brother seeks to defend − or exploit − her. His challenge is recorded − or invented − by Raymond: 'Step down from the tram if you're a man' (48).

When we first read this, we do not know that the brother and sister are Arabs so we interpret the incident as a piece of sexual politics: the struggle for control over women by men. But, before he writes the letter, Meursault learns that Raymond's opponents are Arabs − 'When he told me the woman's name, I saw she was a Moor' (54). So we are invited to reread the previous pages and to interpret them as a piece of colonial politics.

This is reinforced by the way the victories are won: through the use of the French language. First Raymond recounts the battles from his viewpoint using slangy French − 'c'est pas que je suis méchant' (I ain't no trouble-maker) and 'je vais te mûrir' (I'm going to flatten you) − and then Meursault prepares the next onslaught by the written French of his letter. So the languages of the ruling and working classes are fused at the Arab's expense. When in Chapter 4 the state arrives in the shape of the policeman, the punishment inflicted on Raymond is for showing disrespect to him. For his assault on the Arab woman Raymond receives no more than a warning, so the French-Algerian authorities may be said to participate in the brutality. Moreover it is ironic that, when Meursault testifies at the police station, his evidence is accepted, although its only basis lies in the version of events given to him by Raymond. In the second half of the book the authorities will reject Meursault's language, but here the French-Algerian community is drawn together against its common enemy.

The stage is now set for Chapter 6. The Arab is established not merely as agent of the mother, but as antagonist and rival of the pied-noir. Yet this second theme is not fully developed and to explain why, we must have recourse to Michel Foucault's *Discourse on Language*. 'In any society', writes Foucault, 'the production of discourse is controlled, organised, selected and re-arranged by a number of factors which serve to banish the powers and dangers of the discourse' (Foucault, p. 10). In a colonial society, where the prevalent ideology is assimilation, the conflict between colonizer and colonized cannot be treated directly if the legitimacy of the colonizer is not to be undermined. So, if Camus wishes to depict the threat to Meursault's identity, he can only do so via images of sun and sea. The logic in the depiction of the murder of the Arab lies less in what is written than in what is not written.

An Arab is somehow murdered

When asked at his trial, Meursault declares that 'I did not intend to kill the Arab' and that 'it was because of the sun' (158). These replies, which are mocked by the court, must be taken seriously for two reasons. First because their non-intelligibility is an affront to the court's facile rationalism, which is the main theme of Part 2. Secondly because Roland Barthes has argued that the sun is indeed the cause of the murder and that it is the sign of Meursault's adherence to a set of norms different from those observed by society (Barthes, *'L'Etranger*, "roman solaire"', p. 63). This is, however, an odd comment because Barthes seems content to accept the sun as man's destiny without offering any interpretation of what constitutes that destiny.

One such interpretation is that Meursault is a pagan. Robert Champigny writes that Meursault acts in accordance with a nature that has its own coherence. We have already argued that there is certainly a brand of paganism which was inspired by North Africa and which Camus expounds in other books. But it is hard to see what constitutes nature in *The Stranger*. While Chapter 2 and the early pages of Chapter 6 offer a natural world of which Meursault might be considered a part, most of Chapter 6 depicts nothing but the destructive force of a nature that is alien to man. So the question remains: what is the sun and why is it so hostile to Meursault?

The present analysis attempts to make sense of this hostility by using psychoanalytical and political readings. But there remains much in the chapter that cannot be explained. Why does Meursault follow Raymond back to the beach after Raymond's long-time friend Masson decides not to accompany him? Why does Meursault go for the third time to the sun-drenched beach when he is already suffering from the heat? The issue is not to be resolved by mention of the calculated ambiguity which was discussed earlier because Camus, instead of offering no explanation, offers a forceful one: a discourse on the sun composed in lyrical language. However, this discourse is unsatisfactory because it cannot be translated into the language of the rest of the book.

Chapter 6 begins on a contradictory note when Marie tells Meursault that he looks like 'a mourner at a funeral' (77). So the parallels with Chapter 1 are present already. Moreover, the sun resumes its menacing role and strikes Meursault like 'a slap in the face' (77). Then, however, the happiness of the excursion to the beach takes over and the early pages are full of Marie's body-language: her hair hanging free, her laughter, her leaps of joy, the gesture of picking flowers and scattering the petals.

This is followed by other positive indicators. Eating, which is sometimes sordid in *The Stranger*, is joyous here, for lunch consists of fish taken directly from the sea and of bread, which retains in Camus's writing a trace of its sacramental quality. Marie and Meursault swim well, Meursault desires her and there is a moment of joy expressed in language that contains a hint of lyricism: 'we swam away and we felt that we were together in our movements and our happiness' (82).

Of course hints of discord are also present: Marie's dress is coloured white, Raymond does not swim at all, while Masson swims badly and Masson's wife is a Parisian. Yet this is a morning of happiness, when Meursault in an unusual moment thinks about the future. Not only does he discuss renting a cabin on the beach for the summer, but he also realizes that he is soon to be married. There is no reason to suppose that his marriage will be any happier than Salamano's, but this morning represents the kind of life which Meursault will — once he becomes fully aware at the end of the novel — consider the only value in the universe.

The reader is also conscious that this is a French-Algerian day. Most of the elements mentioned — the values of the body, the lack of reflection, the camaraderie and the superficial sense of belonging to nature — are ingredients of pied-noir culture. It follows that the flaw in this happiness will take the form of the Arabs, whom Meursault has already described in a memorable sentence: 'They looked at us in silence but in their way, neither more or less than if we were stones or dead trees' (79).

We are tempted to interpret this by using Sartre's concept of negritude. In colonial societies the vision of the colonizer dominates, and the colonized are obliged to look at themselves as their master does. There comes a moment, however, when the colonized assert their identity against their master by compelling him to submit to their gaze. If this interpretation is true, then Camus is building up the tension in the novel: the 'they', the Arabs, are turning against the 'us', the French-Algerians.

However we are even more struck by the way the Arab's look resembles Meursault's. If the Arab is characterized by indifference — it is here that Camus rejoins the mainstream of French-Algerian writing — then he is another Meursault. Like him, the Arab takes no account of inner life, but rather destroys the elements that are traditionally considered human. He does to Meursault what Meursault had done to the pensioners. Further parallels between the two lie in their cult of silence and their alienation from the values of work and commerce. So not merely does the Arab threaten Meursault because he is the agent of the mother and a rival claimant to the womanhood and land of Algeria, but he is also Meursault's brother, a more authentic Meursault. In this respect, too, he is a menace to Meursault's identity.

After the account of the lunch, the language of the chapter changes and grows ever more lyrical. Sense impressions take on more than physical force, and a hallucination is created where Meursault is brutalized. His enemy is the sun — 'its glare reflected from the sea was unbearable' (85); it is 'overwhelming' (89) and his head 'resounds with sun' (91); the light falls like 'blinding rain' (91). The other objects of nature help to create an inferno: 'heat like stone wells up from the ground' (85), while the sand is 'red-hot' (86). Even the sea betrays Meursault, for 'a dense, fiery breath rises up from it' (95).

Meanwhile time is suspended: 'For two hours the day had not advanced' (93). In the previous sentence the adjective 'same' is repeated three times. Space has shrunk to the beach on which no one is present except the three Europeans and the two Arabs. The sense of ritual is heightened by the use of adjectives like 'equal' and 'regular' (86), while a colour structure is created by the domination of red which is the colour of male sexuality and aggression.

It is more correct to talk of an inferno than of natural objects, because these pages are dominated by what Sartre calls 'word-objects'. They are clustered around the motif of disintegration: 'the sun was breaking itself into pieces on the sand' (89), while two pages later there is 'an explosion of red' (91). And the figure to be destroyed is Meursault: 'all this heat weighed on me and barred my path' (92); a page later the attack comes from the opposite direction — 'an entire beach alive with sunshine pressed me from behind' (93). His existence menaced, Meursault struggles to survive: 'I strained as hard as I could to overcome the sun' (92). The metaphor of the sunlight as a sword-blade is invoked to heighten the danger. As in Chapter 1, but more clearly so, Meursault is near to death.

We are able to link the sun with the Arab in his complementary roles as agent of the mother and enemy of the pied-noir. Each time Meursault goes to the beach, it is to avoid remaining with the women. The first time the reason is the male–female division of labour, where the women remain to wash the dishes. Although the second case is less clear, Meursault's willingness to accompany Raymond may be explained by his dislike of the emotion the women show at Raymond's wound — 'Madame Masson was crying and Marie was very pale' (88). This reminds us of Meursault's refusal to weep at his mother's funeral and also of his refusal to intervene, as Marie asks him to do, when Raymond beats up the Arab woman. So his decision to accompany Raymond marks a rejection of woman in her role as creature of tenderness.

When Meursault returns to the beach for the third time, it is in order not to 'approach the women once more' (91), and later he adds that he is seeking shade to 'flee from the sun, struggle and women's tears' (92). This juxtaposition sums up Meursault's dilemma. If the sun be accepted as an image of the mother, then Meursault is fleeing both the indifferent mother and the tender Marie. He is still unable to free himself from the former by caring for the latter.

But the mother accompanies him to the beach: the colour white is present in the sea-shells which throw back the sun and the colour black in the boat that is out at sea. Moreover, the comparison with the funeral is made via the key adjective 'same': 'It was the same sun as the day when I had buried mother.' Jean Gassin is correct in viewing Meursault's attack on the Arab as a gesture against the mother who is bringing him close to death.

But the political theme is also strong in these pages. Three times the Europeans encounter the Arab amidst a stylized Algerian landscape of sea, sun and sand. The first time the Arabs are victorious and the second time they conquer not by fighting the Europeans but by taking possession of the landscape. 'Quite calm and almost happy' (89), they lie in the sand near a spring and a rock. Where Raymond and even Meursault talk, the Arabs are silent, except that one of them plays three notes on a flute. The flute is significant because it is first described as a reed and thus linked to nature, because music might be considered free from the alienation of verbal communication, and because — as Eisenzweig points out — three constitutes a cycle or a flux but not − at least to Westerners − a progression or a linear development.

To this we might add that three is a key number for Meursault: in Part 2, Chapter 2, he three times repeats the statement that there are things of which he does not like to speak; in the concluding chapter he seems three times to refuse the chaplain, and here there are three meetings on the beach with the Arabs. So this is another parallel between Meursault and his rivals.

Certainly the flute is linked both with silence and the running of the spring: 'the double silence of the flute and the water' (91). Since silence is associated with authenticity, the Arabs are reinforced in their possession not of nature but of the specifically Algerian nature and of its sources of life − water and shade. When he returns the third time Meursault, unable to bear the sun, discovers the single Arab both better able to bear it and sheltered from it: 'his forehead was in the shade of the rock, his body in the sun. His dungarees were smoking in the heat' (92).

So, although Meursault retains sufficient awareness to note that he does not understand what is happening, and although his doubting mind tells him 'it was stupid, I couldn't get rid of the sun by taking one step' (94), *The Stranger* has entered its second lyrical phase and another logic is at work. Meursault must take the shade, the source of life, away from the Arab. Of the battle which follows we note the male sexual overtones: the Arab's knife, which is linked with the sword-blades of the sun, is a phallic symbol, as is Meursault's revolver. So the clash is once more for women and the land of Algeria. Blinded by 'a curtain of tears and salt' (94), Meursault loses even his lingering consciousness, and a fresh onslaught from the sun − 'the sky opened right across to send fire gushing out' (95) − causing him to shoot.

In other books by Camus, like the short-story *Le Renégat*, loss of intellectual clarity and succumbing to absolute belief are the factors that trigger violence. Following this argument, Meursault kills the Arab because he is threatened by a brother-rival whose claim to Algeria is greater than his own.

The piednoir has to kill the Arab — in this sense it is correct to use the term destiny — in order to take possession of the new Mediterranean kingdom. If Meursault is not to die himself, he must carry out the political murder of slaying the Arab.

Had Camus been able to offer a discourse on colonialism that was in Foucault's words 'combative' and liberated from 'taboos' (Foucault, p. 52), then it might have explained how the French-Algerians were, in order to realize themselves as a new culture and people, brutalizing the original occupants of the country. *The Stranger* would have been a sombre warning to Camus's people. It would have dragged into the open the fear of the Arab and the jealousy of an authenticity that is ascribed to him by the European. It would have clarified the relationship between Meursault's resentment of his mother and his vengeance on the Arab.

To say this is, of course, absurd because no such text exists. The thinker whose concept of literature best explains this aspect of *The Stranger* is Pierre Macherey, who argues that a work of fiction is of necessity 'hollow' and 'absent' (Macherey, pp. 75, 97). There can be nothing harmonious that underlie it. Whether or not Macherey's view is generally correct, it offers insights into this work and the settler-colony from which it emerged.

Fear of the Arab, doubts about one's legitimacy and the probability of violence could not be openly stated. So it would be as wrong to explain away the sun as to conclude, as René Girard has done, 'that our efforts to make sense of Meursault's criminal action get nowhere' (Girard, p. 24). We may attempt, in Macherey's words, 'to say what the work does not and could not say' (Macherey, p. 95), namely, the well-nigh impossible historical situation in which French-Algerians found themselves in the late 1930s.

By the 1950s, after the rise of an Arab nationalist movement that offered open opposition to French rule, different literary works could be produced. In *The Exile and the Kingdom* Camus deals somewhat more directly with Arab–European conflicts, and in one of these stories, *The Adulterous Woman*, the Arab is transformed by the French-

Algerian heroine into the incarnation of authenticity.

The Stranger, however, can do no more than point towards the dilemma that French-Algeria was so reluctant to face; the reader must complete the journey himself. It seems to me that it is a red herring to agonize over Camus's attitude towards colonialism. But, if one were to do so, one's first statement would be that he deserves credit for questioning, however obliquely, the ideology of assimilation. That he could not conduct a freer discussion of this taboo and that he could not reconstruct the colony from the viewpoint of the colonized by depicting Arabs as they perceived themselves, merely prove how intractable are the problems posed by a settler-colony.

As for the issue of Meursault's moral responsibility, it is also misplaced. In Part 1, Chapter 6, Meursault is not the free being able to choose between good and evil, who is presupposed by Western legal systems and by the Judaeo-Christian heritage. Even during Chapters 2 to 5 he was not a complete character nor a narrator capable of drawing moral distinctions.

In the last sentence of Chapter 6 comes a moment of awareness: 'I understood that I had destroyed the harmony of the day, the exceptional silence of a beach where I had been happy' (95). As the onslaught of the sun ends, Meursault reasserts himself as an individual and is able to examine the experience he has undergone. There is no reason to think he appreciates the political nature of the Arab's death, but he does understand that the life that has been described in Part 1 is now over, and restrospectively he perceives its value. Significantly, he describes the way it ended as the irruption of sound and hence language into silence.

In a gesture that mingles despair and awareness, he fires four more shots into the Arab's body. The extra shots have greatly preoccupied critics of the novel and we may agree with Eisenzweig's explanation of the number. Four does, unlike three, constitute a linearity rather than a cycle, so the shots mark Meursault's entry into the world of the boss, the warden and the priest.

By firing again he changes the nature of the killing, which

ceases now to be the work of the sun and becomes a common crime. Or so it will appear to the judges, who will see in the extra shots the evidence of a murder that has been deliberately executed. But, since the key shot was the first and since the reader knows that, whatever the crime was, it was not in the conventional sense of the term deliberate, Meursault will remain a man of dissidence and the conflict with authority will now become the main theme. Meursault is imprisoned by the language of authority, as is indicated when he uses the banally literary metaphor of striking 'four rapid blows on the door of misfortune' (95). But if this clash is to become the main theme of Part 2, the relationship between mother and son must be resolved and the dead Arab must vanish, must be murdered all over again.

An Arab forgotten and a mother appeased

The real murder of the Arab takes place now, carried out partly by the state and partly by Meursault. The state's role is obvious: it puts Meursault on trial for not weeping at his mother's funeral. This, Meursault's lawyer tells him, will be 'a mighty argument for the prosecution' (101). And so it proves, for the prosecuting lawyer summons the warden, the caretaker and Pérez to demonstrate Meursault's insensibility and then concludes his cross-examination of the witnesses by declaring that Meursault had 'buried his mother with the heart of a criminal' (148).

Neither the prosecution nor the defence raises the question of why the dead man is an Arab rather than a pied-noir. Indeed, the prosecutor depicts the crime as a settling of accounts among men who are on the fringes of the underworld and are linked with prostitution, while the defence lawyer does not even mention the Arab in his speech. This reflects the official ideology of assimilation, and it is a concerted effort to deny the Arab any existence. Neither the dead man's sister nor his friend is summoned by either side as a witness. Such factors corroborate Eisenzweig's view that the Arab is killed by writing, although this is only part of the explanation and it is true of Part 2 and not of Part 1, Chapter 6.

Another part of the explanation is that in the prison and trial chapters the rivalry and identification between pied-noir and Arab are shrugged off. This is all the more jarring to the reader because the issue is raised in Part 2, Chapter 2:

First of all I was shut in a room where there were several other prisoners, most of them Arabs. They laughed when they saw me. Then they asked what I had done. I told them I had killed an Arab and they were silent. But a moment later it was evening. They showed me how to arrange the mat I was to sleep on. (114)

This is a key paragraph because it reveals the identification between Meursault and the Arab. In a colonial society the prisons will be populated chiefly by the colonized, who will not recognize themselves as criminals guilty of specific crimes but will consider it normal to be in prison. So they welcome Meursault as one of them and, even when he tells them he has killed an Arab, they do not ask for explanations because they do not believe in the pseudo-logic of the French state. In this they are different from the judges and akin to Meursault.

By sleeping in the same way as they do, Meursault becomes, albeit briefly, an Arab. Thus the pied-noir's quest for authenticity is realized, but in a paradoxical manner. A prisoner of the state, he shares the condition of the colonized.

However, the theme is dropped in the same chapter when Marie visits Meursault. Again most of the people present at visiting hour are Arabs, whether prisoners or family. Accustomed to prisons, many of the Arabs communicate despite the noise of the crowd: 'they did not shout. Despite the hubbub they managed to make themselves heard while speaking in low voices' (116). Although Meursault admires this and is troubled by the noise, he and Marie cannot imitate them and Marie has to raise her voice. Thus she and Meursault are once more prisoners of language and separate from the Arabs.

This is the last time that the text shows any awareness of Arabs, and during his trial Meursault asserts his non-comprehension of the murder. Once more it is not a question of the guilt or innocence of the character Meursault, but rather that his guilt or innocence, whichever it may be, is measured by his conflict with the judges. More crudely, Meursault becomes innocent as Part 2 goes on and as the judges are more clearly branded as false. But in this conflict the Arab plays no role at all, his death becoming − like his life and his sister's life − a non-event. He is not even the issue over which Meursault and the judges fight, for that role is monopolized by the mother. The Arab, whose death had some ill-defined political significance in Part 1, Chapter 6, is now a non-person.

This is a further example of what Macherey calls 'hollowness'. For the reader cannot help being aware that something is missing in the text, even if Camus is adept at hiding the void. A contemporary critic, who was writing in the magazine *Confluences*, pointed out that the imposition of the death penalty on Meursault was implausible, because the Arab had a weapon and the murder was perceived by the court as a dispute among criminals. René Girard has stated that the sympathy Meursault wins from the reader is illegitimate because he has, after all, killed a man. Girard ignores the specificity of the Arab, but this is the main theme of Conor Cruise O'Brien's book which argues that no French-Algerian court would ever have condemned a pied-noir to death for killing an armed Arab.

The simplest explanation for the relationship between Part 1, Chapter 6, and Part 2 is given by Brian Fitch, who argues that the murder of the Arab is merely a pretext that allows Meursault to be technically guilty of a crime and hence condemned, while appearing innocent to the reader. Yet the neatness of such a view masks difficult questions. The reason for choosing an Arab as victim would seem then − for the choice must still be explained − that the Western European or North American reader will more easily forgive the murder of an Arab than the murder of a European.

This may indeed be true, for Camus's admirers have demonstrated an extraordinary flair for proving that the Arab's death is 'devoid of all moral significance' (Fitch, *'L'Etranger' d'Albert Camus, un texte*, p. 132). Arab observers might find such zeal misplaced and they might note too that the vast majority of readers in the 1940s, including Sartre, never pose the question of why the death of an Arab furnishes the correct pretext. The short answer is that books are read within historical parameters and, until the outbreak of the Algerian War and more generally of decolonization, criticisms like O'Brien's could scarcely have been made.

From the comfortable vantage-point of the 1980s I am in partial agreement with Fitch: in the second but not the first part of *The Stranger* the murder of the Arab is a pretext that allows Meursault to be condemned while retaining the reader's sympathy. But I also feel that the shift in the murder, which had political significance when committed but becomes non-intelligible later, is felt by the reader as an 'absence'. The shift explains, however, how *The Stranger* was to be read as a novel of the Occupation rather than as a novel of colonialism. But to demonstrate how this took place we must make a detour via the figure of the mother.

Superficially, the evil mother pursues her son throughout Part 2. She has enlisted lawyers and magistrates, who succeeded in punishing him for loving her incestuously – they are the agents of his father – or for not loving her sufficiently – they are her agents. Moreover, Meursault accepts his guilt, as he demonstrates in his interpretation of the text that will become *Le Malentendu*. Although the mother pillages and murders the son, Meursault considers that the son 'had deserved it a bit' (125). So the lawyers and magistrates are the voices of his subconscious, and the incident of the criminal who is to be tried for murdering his father reinforces the theme that Meursault is being tried for murdering his mother. His seeming lack of interest in the trial reflects his desire to follow her into death. For Jean Gassin there is no triumph in the second half of *The Stranger*, which ends with 'the death of the hero who gives up a life that has become impossible because of his mother-fixation' (Gassin, p. 212).

Although this view is plausible, one cannot help agreeing with Fitch, who considers that such a reading ignores the 'intentions of the work' (Fitch, *'L'Etranger' d'Albert Camus, un texte*, p. 89) because it finds Meursault guilty, whereas the text declares him innocent. As already stated in Chapter 1, there is in Camus's writing both admiration and hatred of the mother, and it seems to me that the former dominates in the second half of *The Stranger*. After the colonial issue has been resolved, however inadequately, the mother can switch from being identified with the Arab and can now become her son's ally in his battle with the judges.

His indifference, which becomes less an alienation and more a protest in Part 2, is no longer directed against her; instead, she helps in his struggle against the court's hypocrisy. At first Meursault fights his battle alone: 'I would have preferred that mother not die', he says, and his lawyer 'looked displeased' (102). He loved his mother in the same way as everyone else did, he says, and the court clerk 'mishit the keys of his typewriter' (105). But near the end of his trial Meursault invokes his mother to justify his conduct towards her. Asked yet again if it had not hurt him to place her in a home, he replies that 'neither mother nor I expected anything any longer from each other or from anyone else' (135). So Meursault's indifference is now explicitly presented as a reflection of hers.

This may also explain another aspect of Marie's prison visit. She is flanked by a mother who is visiting her son and by a woman who seems to be the wife of another prisoner. Whereas the wife shouts, the mother and son (the mother dressed in black) look at each other, and she never speaks. Between the two are Marie and Meursault, who are neither mother and son nor husband and wife, and who are forced by the noise to raise their voices. If one follows the language values of *The Stranger*, then the mother–son bond is the deepest and, although Marie does not disappear from the novel after the visit, she does write a letter − the only time she uses the written word outside her work − to say she will not be visiting Meursault again. This might indicate that, as in *The Plague* where Rieux's wife leaves and his mother arrives before the town is sealed, the mother–son relationship dominates.

But it is not perceived as a conflict. Foreshadowing the

reconciliation comes a brief moment of sympathy for the father. Contrasting with the false father-figures of the judge and the priest, Meursault's father appears in the last chapter as an antagonist of the guillotine. Significantly, this story is told via the mother, so that all three family members are drawn together by it. The father attends the execution although 'he felt ill at the idea of going to it' (168). His act is not vulgar sensationalism, but an investigation of capital punishment such as his son will undertake during his meditations in his cell. On his return the father 'had thrown up for part of the morning' (168), thus putting himself in the opposite camp from the judges.

The reconciliation with the mother, which takes up the episode of her evening walks with Pérez, comes in the closing pages. In Part 1, Meursault did not interpret her actions, but here he does: 'So near death, mother must have felt liberated and ready to live everything over again' (185). Her affirmation of life is a model to her son, and she anticipates him as a figure of the absurd.

This theme will be raised in our discussion of the final chapter, but here one may note that the foundations for this reconciliation were laid earlier during the prison and trial chapters, where Meursault's victory over his judges is won by pitting his own and her indifference against the language of authority.

Meursault judges the judges

The structure of Part 2 gives precedence to this conflict, for Chapter 1 depicts the early interrogations of Meursault by his lawyer and the magistrate, while his first days in prison, which take place before these meetings, are reserved for Chapter 2. The chronology of this chapter is blurred and the first page depicts events like Marie's letter which take place after her visit. Since this is the chapter where Meursault repeats that there are things 'I have never liked talking about', we might conclude that Camus wishes to retain something of the doubt that lingered over the narrative form of Part 1.

However, this chapter possesses a clear thematic progression, for it depicts Meursault's evolution during his months in prison and traces a growth in his awareness that prepares us for his attitude during the trial. Chapters 3 and 4 depict the trial, the former ending with Meursault's attempt to distance himself from the court and the latter with the imposition of the death penalty. So not only is Part 2, Chapters 1–4, more like an orthodox journal novel, but its subject is authority versus dissidence.

The outlines are set in Chapter 1. The first questions asked of Meursault have to do with his civil state – his name, address, age and profession. Such details appear arbitrary to him – 'it all seemed like a game' (100) – and the motif of the game versus nature recurs, although it is handled ironically, for Meursault describes the legal system as 'natural' (110). Another recurring motif is the sun which is present in the magistrate's office – 'his office was full of light which was barely filtered by a thin curtain' (103) – and which will grow stronger throughout the trial. Associated again with death, the sun here regains its traditional masculine quality, for it is primarily the agent of the judges.

Writing re-appears in the shape of the clerk who transcribes Meursault's language in this other even more distorted form. The verb 'to understand' is prevalent and, if on page 103 the lawyer cannot understand Meursault, then on page 104 Meursault cannot understand the magistrate. Present too is the strategy of indifference, for Meursault thinks of explaining and defending his point of view to the lawyer before concluding that 'all that didn't really serve much purpose and I gave up the idea out of laziness' (103).

The novelty of Part 2 is that Meursault's indifference ceases to be instinctive and becomes a reasoned world view. Major developments take place in Chapter 2, triggered by Marie's visit, which has already been discussed twice. It remains only to add that, once he receives Marie's letter, Meursault starts to feel 'that I was at home in my cell and that my life stopped there' (115). Now he begins to have 'only a prisoner's thoughts' (120). Learning how to do without cigarettes and sexual pleasure and how to while away the hours, he becomes a model prisoner and yet this adaptation to the world of power is made with great alienation.

This is the sense of the episode of the mess tin whose rounded and hence distorting surface serves as the second mirror of *The Stranger*. If on the first occasion Meursault constituted an image of his mother and had no conscious view of himself, he can here perceive himself but only as someone other than himself: 'it seemed to me that my reflection remained serious even when I tried to smile at it' (126). Awareness is thus accompanied by a form of schizophrenia: the separation of Meursault the model prisoner from another, freer Meursault.

His true character is discovered a moment later: 'But at the same time and for the first time in months I distinctly heard the sound of my voice. I recognized it as the one that had been ringing in my ears throughout long days, and I understood that for all that time I had been talking to myself' (126). This is the monologue which cannot be written down and of which *The Stranger* is a faint echo. Its content is 'the hour without a name' (126), the horrors of evenings in prison as recognized by the Meursault who is still, in spite of what he said earlier, a free man. This unwritten text does find its way into Chapter 3, where Meursault will be able to describe the evenings of his former life, the value of which he is now better able to appreciate.

During the trial chapters his sense of the conflict between his freedom and the power of the state grows. At the outset he has the 'bizarre impression that I was superfluous, a bit like a gatecrasher' (130). Then he finds an ally in one of the journalists who is conspicuously unlike the others. As stated in Chapter 1, Camus was a self-critical journalist and in *The Stranger* he satirizes the reporters who have 'played up' (130) Meursault's case. The worst of them is the Parisian, but there is one who is not carrying his fountain pen and who is thus not participating in the pseudo-objectivity of the others. Indeed he is, like Rambert in *The Plague*, not writing at all.

This is the one whom Meursault looks at and whose eyes he can perceive. When the journalist looks at Meursault — as he will do until the death sentence is pronounced — Meursault has 'the bizarre impression of being looked at by myself' (132). This is not a case of fraternity but rather one where this non-journalist confirms in Meursault the new awareness of himself as an outsider, who does not fit the categories of prisoner or murderer to which the other journalists and the lawyers have relegated him.

The sense of fraternity comes in Chapter 3 when Meursault has quite different reactions to the prosecuting lawyer and to Céleste. Each time he seems surprised at his own emotion. When the lawyer triumphs, Meursault notes: 'I had a stupid urge to weep, because I felt how much all these people detested me' (138). If the verb 'to feel' is significant, his reaction to Céleste's evidence is stronger: 'I said nothing . . . but for the first time in my life I wanted to kiss a man' (143). In this sentence lie the reaffirmation of silence as honesty, a moment of working-class solidarity and an unusual emotion.

At the end of Chapter 3 Meursault begins to separate himself from the court and to assert his other identity: his kinship with the Meursault of Part 1. It is now that he remembers the Algiers evenings: 'all of the familiar sounds of a town I loved and of a particular time of day when I often felt happy' (148). He then lists concrete impressions such as the cries of newspaper vendors (a form of language that is resolutely unsophisticated) because he does not attempt to idealize or dramatize the life he had lived. Rather it is the immediate experience, uncluttered by intellectual categories, that he asserts, even if the act of assertion is intellectual.

Concomitantly, Meursault withdraws from his trial as he perceives that it has nothing to do with him: 'Everything was unfolding without any intervention from me. My fate was being decided without my opinion being asked' (151). The mechanism by which this takes place will be discussed later, but in Chapter 4 Meursault is able to explain that mechanism, and before the death penalty is announced he has already abandoned the identity of Meursault, the murderer-on-trial: 'the uselessness of what I was doing there welled up in my throat' (161). By now his other identity is fully developed, built out of concrete memories: 'the smells of summer, the neighbourhood that I liked, an evening sky, Marie's laughter and her dresses' (161). So, when the death penalty is pronounced, he has already circumvented it.

It is this Meursault who as well as escaping also vanquishes the judges by imposing his language on theirs, thus revenging the defeat suffered at the trial by his working-class friends, whose language is shattered by the false rationalism of the court.

Even before they begin to speak, Céleste, Marie, Salamano, Masson and Raymond are out-of-place. Céleste has put on the suit that he wears to race-tracks (another association between sport and happiness), while Marie is obliged to hide her long hair under a hat, the values of the body having no place in the courtroom where her sexuality is perceived as a crime. The declarations which the friends make reiterate basic tenets of working-class culture: friendship, solidarity, fatalism and resignation. Nowhere in this culture is there the sense that the universe may be understood, which is the significance of Salamano's comment: 'You have to understand' (145). The judges cannot understand that Salamano means the opposite of what he is saying, namely, that there are areas of life that lie beyond human comprehension and judgement and that must therefore be treated with sympathy.

Both Céleste and Raymond reiterate the non-intelligibility of the crime, Céleste describing it as a 'misfortune' (142) and Raymond as the fruit of 'chance' (146). Each time these non-explanations are dismissed by the court which is too busy constructing its own false explanations. Céleste goes farther by expanding in his inarticulate way on other values of working-class life. When asked whether Meursault was his 'customer', he replies that Meursault was also his 'friend' (141), thus transforming the economic relationship of commerce into a personal one. The stress on friendship, even in the debased form that Raymond represents, is a yardstick by which to measure the insincerity of the court, which condemns Meursault for not mourning his mother with the appropriate external signs of emotion.

Céleste raises another conflict when he declares that Meursault is 'a man' and adds that 'everyone knew what that meant' (141). This is a plea for the universality of Céleste's values, and the irony is that it is rejected by a bourgeois court which is itself pleading the universality of such values as legal guilt or innocence.

Class conflict is sharp at this moment, but the court's victory is complete. By his cross-examination of Marie, the state's lawyer turns her relationship with Meursault into a shameful 'irregular liaison' (144), thus re-establishing traditional taboos on sexuality and branding Marie as little more than a prostitute (and hence linking her with the Arab woman). Her sobs reveal her understanding of what is happening – 'she said it wasn't that at all, it was something quite different, she was being forced to say the opposite of what she thought' (145).

The language of the lawyers is a banal – perhaps too banal – rhetoric. Addresses to the jury abound, as do questions that require no answers and emotive adjectives like 'sacred' (156), 'squalid' (147) and 'sordid' (147); such adjectives are frequently used in the superlative – 'the lowest kind' and 'the most shameful debauchery' (147), and 'the most abominable of crimes' (156). The defence lawyer uses similar language and displays adjectives that are mirror images of the prosecution's. So Meursault is described as 'honest', 'reliable', 'indefatigable', 'faithful' and 'sympathetic' (159). The ingredient of authority in this language comes from the fact that its emotional tone admits of no reply. Not only is it, as stated earlier, akin to the telegram in that it is remote from concrete experience, but it flaunts its own preconceived judgements. Of these there are two which form part of the state's ideology: that men are primarily spiritual beings endowed with souls and that men's actions possess a coherence.

Sartre's view of souls, which was quoted in Chapter 1, might be the best comment on the perorations which both lawyers make about Meursault's soul. Significantly, neither of them has any trouble comprehending it but, whereas the prosecution finds in it 'nothing human' (153), the defence discovers 'a model son' (160). This satire on the idealization practised by society prepares for the second myth: the supposed coherence of human behaviour.

Once more defence and prosecution agree, demonstrating that the conflict is never between them but between Meursault and the entire court. The defence argues that the crime was 'a moment of aberration' (161) in a life that otherwise possesses a clear logic. Incoherence may then be admitted, if it declares itself as such, does not last long and expects to be treated as if it were coherent. The lawyer does not declare that Meursault should not be punished or that he should not feel remorse. As for the prosecution, it reconstructs a Meursault who shows no trace of incoherence. He is a hardened criminal who refuses to weep at his mother's funeral, engages in irregular liaisons the next day, has underworld connections and commits a premeditated murder. One remembers Barthes's view that the death of the Arab is left unexplained precisely in order to accentuate the conflicts between Meursault and society. While it has been argued that this is not true of Part 1, Chapter 6, it is a correct interpretation of Part 2. One is also reminded that in the *Discourse on Language* Foucault warns us against the quest for causality and suggests that an important part of any discourse lies in its 'discontinuity' (Foucault, p. 54).

The view that Meursault acted while 'knowing exactly what he was doing' (153) receives support from the extra four shots which must be considered again. They are the crux of the discussion in Part 2, Chapter 1, with the magistrate. Following Eisenzweig's interpretation, the four shots are the first sign that Meursault is entering the world of rationality and power; if this is precisely the aspect of his crime that is held against him, it is because society does not wish to recognize itself for what it is but rather perceives its version of reason as universal and of power as justice. To this one might add two small footnotes. First, in confirmation of Eisenzweig's interpretation of the number four, we may remark that the magistrate repeats the word 'why' four times (106), when he asks about the extra shots. Secondly it is revealing once again that the magistrate ignores the specificity of the Arab to concentrate on a statistic — the number of shots. In response, Meursault says nothing but thinks that the point 'was not very important' (107), indicating already that the trial will be fought over false issues, over the four shots rather than over the first shot and the sun.

Another way to consider the interpretations of the lawyers is as stories, pieces of fiction made up for the jury and public, with the journalists as book-reviewers. As such they are the kind of fiction that Camus and Sartre most disliked: omniscient authors have created a puppet-character called the murderer, Meursault, who is allowed no freedom and is to be justly punished. Meursault invites us to consider the trial in this way, for he notes — in his role as reader of such fiction — that the prosecutor's way of 'looking at the events did not lack clarity. What he was saying was plausible' (153). The difference between the puppet-character and Camus's character-narrator is that, whereas the former has no language, the latter does and he uses it adroitly. His aim is to undermine the lawyers' fiction by irony, and to reappropriate the power they exert over him by relaying their rhetoric in the form of free indirect speech.

This is a conscious attempt, because Meursault knows that he is being guillotined in advance by the lawyers' language. The defender uses 'I' when he means Meursault, who comments: 'I thought it was removing me from the whole business and reducing me to nothing' (159). So Meursault launches a counter-attack and avenges his friends Céleste and Marie. Indeed it may not be too exaggerated to see in the pages that depict them a critique of another kind of fiction: populism. Their shortcomings are precisely those which characterize populist writing: sentimentality, defeatism and a sense of its own illegitimacy in the face of high culture. If this be so, then Meursault's discourse is both more radical and more sophisticated, deploying irony as its weapon.

Free indirect speech is a third form that stands beside direct and indirect speech. Instead of 'I wish to leave' or 'he said that he wished to leave', one may use 'he wished to leave'.

More interestingly, free indirect speech is a case where the speaker does not appear in his own right as an 'I' and does not use his own language. Nor does he appear as the autonomous author – the 'he said that' – of his statements. Indeed, these appear on the surface to have no author. But, although this supports Barthes's view that the language of *The Stranger* is 'neutral', the phenomenon of the seemingly absent author is more complex.

Direct speech is usually a sign that experience is being transmitted with immediacy. In *The Stranger* there is comparatively little direct speech, which confirms the conclusion that even in the first half of the book Meursault is a creature of frustrated awareness rather than a thoughtless barbarian. Not surprisingly, there is a great deal of indirect speech where the 'he said' reminds the reader that experience is being filtered through language. But free indirect speech allows the filtering to be done not by the character himself but by someone else, which undermines the character's autonomy.

When the boss asks Meursault to go to Paris, all three kinds of speech are used: 'He declared that he was going to talk to me about a plan that was still vague . . .' (indirect speech); 'he intended to set up an office in Paris that would conduct his business on the spot and directly with the big companies . . .' (free indirect speech); '"You are young and it seems to me a life you would like"' (direct speech) (68). By using free indirect speech for the middle and most important section, Camus weakens the validity of the plan, which is then more convincingly rejected by Meursault.

It is no coincidence that the boss is a figure of power, because free indirect speech is used chiefly in the second half of the book and its goal is, as Fitch has pointed out, to deflate the lawyers' rhetoric. In one passage Meursault ironically reclaims the 'I' that is elsewhere appropriated by the defence lawyer. The prosecutor 'declared to the jury that it was generally known that the witness exercized the profession of a pimp. I was his accomplice and his friend. The whole business was a squalid intrigue of the lowest kind' (147). Here the 'I' reminds the reader that the narrator is not the lawyer but Meursault, who is mimicking the lawyer's words. Not only does this point out the pomposity of 'squalid' and 'lowest', but it creates a comic effect because Meursault is allowing himself to be castigated.

Free indirect speech does not remove the author, but it enables him to exert a subtle power over the speaker. Since Meursault, the character, is in a position of weakness, his assertion of power via his role as narrator is all the more striking. No longer are the representatives of the state in control of what they say; instead they become comic characters in the work of fiction that Meursault is offering us. Their creations of a Meursault who premeditated his crime or was a model son are unconvincing alongside his creations of pompous men using meaningless language.

This is why the ambiguity of Part 1 gives way to a self-assured irony. Meursault's language is no longer interrogating itself; rather its lack of certainty becomes the sane vantage-point from which one laughs at the presumptuous antics of the judges. The second half of *The Stranger* may be read as a comic novel. Meursault's ability to find anything and everything interesting always had possibilities for humour, but they are not exploited until these chapters. 'Even when you're in the dock it's always interesting to hear yourself talked about' (151) is a sentence that mocks the court's sacrosanct aura, while placing Meursault, the humorist, outside the dock. His willingness to approve of a legal system that is so clearly absurd reinforces that absurdity: 'I had to give the details of who I was all over again and, although I was annoyed, I thought it was really pretty natural because to judge one man in place of another would be very serious' (134). Best of all is Meursault's reply when told that the magistrate will name a defence lawyer: 'I thought it was very convenient that the justice system should take care of these details. I said this to him. He agreed and concluded that the law worked well' (100).

By such comedy Meursault wins the reader's sympathy. Dissidence defies authority and, if the contemporary reader can still not quite forget that somehow an Arab has been murdered, he is certain that the judges are guilty and Meursault innocent. As Fitch points out, Meursault becomes 'our spiritual brother' (Fitch, *Narrateur et narration dans 'L'Etranger'*, p. 58). One may see at least one reason why *The Stranger* was so widely read during the Occupation. At a time when French institutions had lost their legitimacy and when the legal system was perverted by the Nazi invaders and the Vichy regime to brand the Resistants as terrorists, Camus's satire had great appeal.

The reader's only reserve is that Meursault's victory is rather too easily won. Critics who accept the notion of probability are correct to argue that no court would have condemned a man to death for not weeping at his mother's funeral. Even critics who refuse to stray from the text must surely feel that the lawyers' rhetoric is inflated, and that the magistrate who marches around his office with a crucifix that he had pulled from his filing cabinet is too grotesque a figure. Fitch wonders whether the narrator, Meursault, would be capable of such irony and whether some of the more comic passages are not written by a cleverer man called Camus. One tends to agree, especially since Meursault's awareness of the trap into which he has fallen grows slowly from Chapter 2 on, whereas the passage about the law working well comes from Chapter 1.

These are, however, minor objections and the last one may be inherent in the genre of the journal-novel. By the end of Chapter 4, Meursault is established as the man who lives honestly and who is victimized by an oppressive, falsely humanistic society. This theme will receive further development in the last chapter, where Meursault must face death not in its social guise — the death penalty imposed by unjust men — but as the great fact of the human condition.

God is dead and Existentialism is born

The final chapter has been described by one critic as 'an interpretation of what has preceded, a summing up of the knowledge gained' (Viggiani, p. 885). The allusions to fatality which are scattered throughout the book take shape in what Meursault called 'the mechanism' that will terminate his existence. In Part 1 death was wrapped in lyricism and, while Meursault the character was saved because others died in his stead, Meursault the narrator defended himself with his ambiguity. There is no such ambiguity in the last chapter, nor is there much irony, for Meursault can no longer outwit his enemies by humour. Now he has to find a new language and in fact he discovers two: an attempted meditation on his own extinction and a cry of revolt.

There is fresh doubt about the sequence of this chapter because the first page is written in the present tense, which leads Fitch to argue that it is chronologically the last moment of the book, that the interview with the priest has already taken place and that Meursault is now writing his journal. This may well be true, although one remembers that *The Stranger* takes some care to prevent us from understanding when and how it has been written. As for this chapter, it may be read, as Viggiani has suggested, as a separate entity where unity lies in the clash of extremes: the way that an extremely intellectual discourse breaks down and triggers an emotional outburst.

The number three stands at the outset − 'For the third time I refused to receive the chaplain' (165) − to remind us that we are outside history and that the political struggle of Part 2, Chapters 1–4, is over. Meursault's awareness has grown and he is focusing it on his forthcoming end. He himself puts it differently: 'What interests me at this moment is to escape the mechanism' (165). But the trouble is that he cannot escape it and the structure of his meditation is that a cycle is repeated five times. Each time Meursault seeks to divert his mind from death but each time he is brought back to it.

The first time he thinks of escape and spins out a tale of books on escape − fabulous, unread and unwritten texts that depict last-minute flights − and then he concludes: 'But, all things considered, nothing allowed this luxury, everything denied it to me, the mechanism took hold of me again' (166). The difference between this language and the rest of the book is that doubt has now vanished. The usual formula of 'all things considered', which used to announce an awareness stranded in uncertainty, here announces the categorical statement emphasized by words 'nothing' and 'everything'. Meursault has attained certainty by coming up against his own limits.

Unable to confront this — 'despite my good will I could not accept this insolent certainty' (167) — he spins out a second flight which avoids the imminence of death by demonstrating that the penalty was imposed arbitrarily; but this tale has as its conclusion that, arbitrary or not, the decision is final. There follow similar tales where Meursault imagines that he is a spectator at the execution, that the guillotine might not work or that, since it is high above the ground, it is an imposing and noble edifice.

It is not fanciful to suggest that Camus is here explaining the ground rules of his own fiction, which refuses to accept the imaginative 'world' as the equivalent of reality. By using the language of analytical thought — the guillotine is described as 'a work of precision' (170) — he undercuts the tale-telling of traditional novels. Meursault, who has always distrusted imagination, is thrown back on reason which offers him, however, an equally unsatisfactory discourse.

His next subterfuge is to plunge into his fear: 'the most reasonable thing was not to force myself' (171). Yet he retains control, even if the reader feels already that the breakdown is near. First Meursault imposes on his mind the target of surviving past dawn — prisoners to be executed are taken out at dawn — and then during the day he juggles with his appeal, imagining now that it is accepted and now that it is rejected. The distinctive feature of these exercises is their intellectual rigour, which is forced on the reader's attention even as its tenuous control is equally stressed: 'Therefore (and the difficult thing was not losing sight of all the reasoning that this "therefore" represented)' (174).

Meursault's task, which is also depicted in *La Mort heureuse* and which will be discussed in the next chapter, is to compel his sane mind to face death. Whereas most people combat death with the consolations of having played a role in a larger historical process or of perpetuating themselves biologically via their children, Meursault confronts it alone. Whereas most people are racked with pain, bewildered by age or befuddled with drugs, Meursault is healthy, young and in full possession of his faculties. His loneliness is accentuated by the way he specifically rejected Marie − 'outside of our two bodies which were now separated nothing bound us together' (175). Indeed it is because this meditation refuses the usual non-transcendental forms of consolation that it forces the reader back to God and constitutes − in my opinion − religious writing.

Meursault's rigour is designed to compel man, a creature defined by his desire for immortality, to confront his mortality. This is what Camus will call 'the absurd' in *The Myth of Sisyphus*, where the confrontation will be handled differently. Here Meursault is tested by his conversation with the priest.

Although he enters without permission and although he is yet another false father, the priest is not to be dismissed as a mere adjunct of the state. The conversation of Part 2, Chapter 1, depicts the crucifix-wielding magistrate as a false priest who deploys clichés. In a banal parody of pious jargon he invites Meursault to become 'a child whose soul is empty and ready to welcome anything' (107). But this time the priest is not to be dismissed with easy irony.

He offers two kinds of arguments: the existence of sin and the impossibility of a world without God. In secularizing the concept of sin, by refusing to admit anything more than that society considers him guilty, Meursault is rejecting the framework of theological values that embraces sin. The term has no meaning unless one also believes not merely in free will but in grace and forgiveness, which in turn presupposes a loving God. This leads easily to the affirmation (shared by Camus) that God does not exist and to a further affirmation (unshared by Camus) that desire for immortality is 'no more important than wanting to be rich, to be able to swim very fast or to have a better-shaped mouth' (181).

Against transcendental values, Meursault asserts the kind of life he had lived in Part 1 and of which he became gradually aware in Part 2, Chapters 1–4. When the priest asks him to perceive in the prison stones 'a divine face' (180), Meursault replies that he has only ever seen there Marie's face and that he can now see only the stone. Stone, which is in Camus's work associated both with happiness and distress, is here an image of earthly life, and this is the life which Meursault asserts against the priest. Enraged at the illusion he is being offered, he breaks into the cry: 'Something broke inside me and I started crying at the top of my voice' (182). Like the Arab woman, he begins with a denunciation, when he insults the priest and insists that he does not want to be prayed for.

The language of this cry is a variation on ordinary rhetoric. Questions, repetitions and antitheses abound although the clauses are short and the vocabulary is simple. The weakness of these pages lends credence to Gassin's contention that the book's ending is not convincing, although one might argue that this discourse should be read not for itself but as the metaphor of a cry which cannot exist inside the pages of a book, and which is echoed by the 'cries of hatred' with which society will greet Meursault's execution.

After denouncing the priest, Meursault repudiates as intellectualizations all judgements, whether moral or religious. The verb 'to understand' is used in a new sense. It is the priest who is being challenged and who fails to understand – 'Did he understand, did he understand this?' (184) – while Meursault is in possession of wisdom. This consists in being able to articulate a preference for the flux of sensory experience and a refusal to categorize: 'I had lived in one way and I could have lived in another. I had this and I had not done that. I had not done one thing while I had done another. So what?' (183).

The Stranger ends as Meursault affirms the worth of his daily round on the Algiers streets, a life that is both alienated because of the seeming absence of values and honest in its refusal of illusions. Non-intelligibility is changed by the act of recognizing and choosing it. In this way *The Stranger* offers the reader an early version of French Existentialism, which further explains the book's success.

But if this is the last word of such an elusive text, then it must be qualified in two ways. First, a wisdom that involves reflection on as well as involvement in concrete existence will surely strive to draw values from that reflection. *The Stranger* ends with an outburst where the simplicity of the language is a barrier against this development, but elsewhere such wisdom must spawn new moralities and ideologies. This will take place in Camus's other books, especially in *The Myth of Sisyphus*.

The second qualification is present in *The Stranger* itself and has to do with the vexing issue of oneness. In the last two pages the lyrical language returns and sensations of light, noise and smell take on a significance that is more than physical: 'Sounds of the countryside rose up to me. Odours of night, earth and salt refreshed my face. The marvellous peace of this sleeping summer came flooding over me' (185). This is different from the images of Part 1, Chapters 1 and 6, for no terror is involved and nature is not hostile, but is in sympathy with Meursault's revolt against the priest. Indeed it contains a language that is intelligible to him: 'in the face of this night full of signs and stars I opened myself for the first time to the tender indifference of the world' (185).

So the experience of oneness marks not merely that death is near but that some kind of truth or harmony has been attained. Meursault does not develop this theme and the lyrical vein is less strong than in the earlier passages. Moreover, he ends on a note of dualism, because he imagines himself going to the guillotine amidst the cries of hatred. However, the special insight into his condition which he expresses in these last pages is linked with the moment of oneness.

Hard as it is for me to define this experience with simple language and without injecting into it religious content, it is equally hard not to believe that Meursault's statement that the desire for God is no more important than desiring to swim well is misleading. It is the awareness of some sort of harmony that enables Meursault to appreciate both the happiness and the shortcomings of his absurd existence. This is surely why he compares himself with Christ on the final page: 'So that all may be consumated' (185).

Christ was God and man, and Camus believed he was chiefly the latter. But Christ is an uninteresting figure unless He retains some tiny trace of the Godhead, and this trace is what lurks behind the 'night full of signs'. At the very least the absence of God is not to be forgotten or overcome. And this in turn means that the final chapter of *The Stranger* does not merely sum up the rest of the book — and does not really fit with Part 1, Chapters 1 and 6 — but looks outward to Camus's other books.

Chapter 3

Early Camus and Sartre

As stated in Chapter 1, Camus considered that *The Stranger*, *Caligula* and *The Myth of Sisyphus* should be read together, because they make up the cycle of the absurd. However, Camus also writes in *The Myth* that the works of an absurd artist may seem 'to have no connection one with the others' (*OC* 2,190). *Caligula* has few significant links with *The Stranger* and hence we shall treat it briefly. *The Myth* will be discussed at greater length because it takes up the issues of Meursault's growing awareness and of the religious motif in the last chapter. Indeed it will be argued that *The Myth* represents both a conclusion and an interpretation of *The Stranger*, even if its interpretation resolves in an unsatisfactory manner the ambiguity of Part 1.

There are contrasts and parallels between *The Stranger* and Sartre's early fiction, *Nausea* (1938) and *The Wall* (1939). While Camus recognized the kinship between his sense of the absurd and that of Sartre, the differences between them were great and the origins of their famous quarrel in 1952 may be traced to their early writing. A glance at Camus's other books and at the young Sartre enables us better to situate *The Stranger*.

The cycle of the absurd

Caligula does not belong entirely to the same period of Camus's writing as *The Stranger* and *The Myth*, because it was revised in 1944, 1947 and 1957. The impact of the Second World War led Camus to emphasize his condemnation of Caligula's brutality and to strengthen the role of the emperor's antagonist, Cherea. At the time when Camus was writing *The Stranger*, Caligula may have been an even more problematic figure than in the 1957 version.

Superficial parallels between novel and play abound. In *Caligula* the figure of the mother recurs: Act 1 begins with Drusilla's death (as a sister with whom the emperor had an incestuous affair, she reminds us of Meursault's mother) and near the end of the play Caligula murders Caesonia (who is both mistress and mother and whose death reminds us of Meursault's 'matricide'). *Caligula* contains a radical political discourse which reminds us of the class conflicts in *The Stranger*. The emperor notes that 'governing is stealing' (*OC* 1,22), and the freed slave Hélicon denounces virtue and justice as fictions that mask oppression. Although this is not the main political theme of *Caligula*, it echoes the satire of the judges in *The Stranger*.

Yet Caligula and Meursault are very different, for Caligula is haunted by the absolute: 'This world, as it is made, is unbearable. So I need the moon or happiness or immortality or something else which may be mad but is not of this world' (15). Such remarks are the antithesis of Meursault's assertion that the stones of the earth and Marie's body are sufficient for him.

Instead of combating his need for immortality, Caligula seeks to become God by assuming the divine prerogative of taking human life. His version of immortality is 'the unlimited joy of the unpunished assassin' (06). At the end he offers his self-critique – 'killing is no solution' (107) – but he then acquiesces in his own assassination. Murder and suicide are the twin poles of his existence and, once more, they are the opposite of Meursault's desire to live.

If we move from the *characters* Meursault and Caligula to the narrator Meursault and the dramatist Caligula, we see more interesting links between Camus's fiction and his theatre. In both cases his aim was to disturb the reader-spectator and to prevent him from identifying with a hero or entering a story.

Caligula is not merely an emperor but an actor, stage-manager and dramatist who from Act 2 to Act 4 offers the city of Rome a piece of theatre: 'I invite you to a limitless feast, to a mass trial, to the finest of shows. I need people, spectators, victims and villains' (28).

Although the sinister allusion to a trial reminds us that Camus lived in the age of show trials, the audience is partially won over by Caligula's theatre. It laughs with him and at the patricians as he strips away the hypocrisy behind which they conceal their privileges. Caligula is engaged in demythologization: in undercutting the gods and institutions of Rome and also the conventions of the theatre.

The issue of how the audience is supposed to react to the play becomes the main theme, because this self-aware work is littered with characters who are artists, with plays within the play, with poetry competitions and with aesthetic discussions. It also has its own audience within the play: the patricians, Scipion, Cherea, Hélicon and Caesonia.

When we remember that *Caligula* was originally written for Camus's troupe, we are not surprised that the spectators' reactions are mixed. They run the gamut from Hélicon's sympathy to Cherea's rebellion. But the most interesting spectator is Scipion, who is unable to formulate a coherent attitude because he is torn between loving and loathing Caligula.

This is, of course, different from the ambiguity that marks Part 1 of *The Stranger*. The spectator is not left without explanations, so he does not feel that Caligula remains unknown to him as Meursault did. Instead, he feels the emotional reaction that Camus considered necessary in the theatre. Still, this reaction is as mixed as Scipion's: sympathy for Caligula's anguish and disgust at his brutality; admiration for the satire in Caligula's theatre and irritation at the dramatist who forces his work on a captive audience. So the spectator's position is as uncomfortable as the position of Meursault's readers, and we are reminded of Jean Grenier's comment − quoted in Chapter 1 − on the parallels between Camus's novel and his theatre.

The Myth of Sisyphus, however, offers explanations for Meursault. To complicate matters further Camus accepted some of them and used them as the springboard for the next phase of his work: *The Plague*, *The Rebel* and *The Just*, which make up the cycle of revolt. Yet, as well as displaying the inevitable differences between a novel and an essay,

The Stranger and *The Myth* depict the absurd differently, *The Myth* presenting it, so I shall argue, in a religious context.

It begins with the by now familiar issues of language and genre. The topic of the absurd is one where 'classical dialectic' must give way to 'common sense and sympathy' (*OC* 2,100). Can a philosophical treatise, Camus wonders, be written about a topic that defies philosophy? He resolves the matter in two ways. He claims that he is writing with 'common sense', because he is dealing with the practical matter of whether the absurd should lead man to suicide. But he admits that 'classical dialectic' cannot be banished, because man cannot prevent himself from analysing and making judgements. Indeed, his inability to do so is part of the absurd. So, although Camus says that he is describing an absurd sensibility rather than analysing the concept of the absurd, he is not unwilling to admit that is doing both. *The Myth* is description-analysis; it is an essay-treatise. If this displeases philosophers, Camus might have written, then so much the worse for them. However, Camus cannot avoid the fact that, as the essay goes on, he changes the absurd by analysing it.

In the early pages he writes: 'I said that the world is absurd but I was going too fast. In itself the world is not reasonable, that is all one can say. What is absurd is the confrontation between the irrational and the frenzied desire for clarity that springs from the depths of man's being. The absurd depends as much on man as on the world' (113). To a tree the universe is not absurd for the tree has its place; the universe is absurd to man who has no place and is tormented by a 'nostalgia for unity' and a 'hunger for the absolute' (110).

Camus lists examples of the absurd that are generally reminiscent of *The Stranger*: the daily routine of work, which is rendered tolerable by habit, can trigger an onrush of futility (we remember Meursault's comments on work in Part 1, Chapter 1); man lives for the future but ahead of him lies nothing but death (Meursault talking to the boss about careers); a landscape may by its very beauty indicate its indifference to man (Meursault on the hills around Marengo); a man speaking in a phone booth seems to the observer a puppet making empty gestures (to Meursault, most people appear in this light).

These examples revolve around the antithesis of man's determination to see in the universe a reflection of himself and the universe's inability to resemble him. It is important to understand the nature of the demand that Camusian man is making. He is asking for certainty: not intellectual knowledge, but the feeling that he is part of a greater intelligence, which means an emotional and spiritual bond with some sort of God.

This is why Camus can write that no scientific comprehension can satisfy man and that 'to understand is above all to unify'. Even reason is identified with the hunger for the absolute − 'man's thought is above all his nostalgia' (134). Psychoanalytical and historical interpretations of the human condition are as irrelevant as science, which leaves only religion.

However, *The Myth* goes on to argue that religion offers a false solution. Camus lists the thinkers who have taken leaps of faith that are mere forms of suicide. The early Existentialist, Karl Jaspers, the phenomenologists Husserl and Heidegger, Kierkegaard, Dostoyevsky, Shestov and Kafka are scrutinized and rebuked. Camus praises them for asserting that the world cannot be explained by reason, but berates them for then deciding to embrace the irrational. The reader may be surprised at seeing so many different artists and philosophers lumped together in a fairly brief discussion (although these are the names that crop up everywhere in 1940s' French writing), but Camus is using them to illustrate his central theme. Man needs the totality which only religion professes to offer, but religion cannot really offer it.

One of Camus's friends, Louis Bénisti, said that the young Camus was not an atheist nor even an agnostic, but that he believed in 'a God of whom you could ask nothing'. So the curious entity that Camus calls man is defined by his need for an absent God. But since this need cannot be satisfied, why should man not try to shrug it off and concentrate on history

or psychoanalysis? Certainly not, replies Camus. The attempt
to satisfy the need for God is indeed a sickness or a suicide,
but the need, which we might redefine as the capacity to be
aware of the divine, can become a positive force. It involves
a dual act of defiance in that man spurns the false explanations of the world that are offered by judges and govern-
ments, and also in that he refuses to yield to the need itself.
Although the absurd may now be redefined as a defiance of
the godhead, it remains a form of religious experience
because it stems from man's awareness of the godhead.
Without what Camus calls nostalgia, the absurd − that non-
meeting of man and the universe − could not take place.

Before we trace the positive implications of the absurd, we
must return to *The Stranger* and consider how our interpretation of it is affected by our reading of *The Myth*. First, if the
religious urge involves the temptation of suicide, we may
brood, retrospectively, on the figures of the mother and the
Arab. Might they not possess − along with their
psychoanalytical and political associations − religious
elements before which Meursault recoils?

More importantly, the trace of the godhead that was present in the last chapter has grown clearer in *The Myth*, and
we might reread the passage about 'the night full of signs'.
The absurd existence, which Meursault has learned to value,
is happy because of these signs, which are the signs not of the
night but of his nostalgia. Already in *The Stranger* the absurd
was acquiring a shape and a coherence.

The second half of *The Myth* spells out what this coherence
might be. The 'heartrending, marvellous gamble of the absurd' (137) lies in the lucid refusal of reconciliation with the
universe. Key words in *The Myth* are 'enumerate' (in contrast
with 'explain') and 'quantity' (in contrast with 'quality').
Since there is no causality, experiences must be listed rather
than re-arranged into an order. Since there are no qualitative
distinctions, choices are to be made by quantity. It is not
better, for example, to be an actor than to be a judge; a man
can merely act or judge with greater or lesser intensity. Yet
here again Camus suggests two or three ways of organizing

experience, which emerge from the lucidity that is inherent in the absurd. Man may become *homo ludens* or he may create new moral values.

If the universe offers no values, life can be a game or a play. Camus offers as a model the actor who feels no emotions but mimes them all, who combines intensity with distance, and who acquires a large quantity and diversity of experience. He may be Hamlet and Prometheus on successive nights. If he so wishes, he may be Hamlet offstage as well as onstage, because the stable human personality is an illusion.

Another model is Don Juan, who plays out the game of seduction. Reversing the traditional notion that Don Juan is the man in pursuit of an ideal love, Camus defines him as not believing in love and simply seducing a number and variety of women. The word 'simply' is significant because Don Juan is not a complex or a superior figure; there can be little complexity and no heroes in a world where there are no hierarchies of values.

Yet the second code outlined in *The Myth* involves the rebirth of moral values. There are two very different directions in Camus's moral thinking. Having stressed common sense at the outset, he goes on to invoke the body. Although it suffers from the absurd – this is what constitutes 'nausea' – the body refuses its own extinction in suicide. So it is a source of wisdom and, if man follows its suggestions, it will lead him to happiness. Just as *The Stranger* emphasized the body's grace, *The Myth* shows its health and sanity. They lead man to reject the aberrations of his mind, and they guide him towards what we might call the morality of happiness. Man can enjoy his own sexuality and the beauty of the natural world; he will avoid extremes; he will trust in his instincts.

Implicitly – in *The Plague* it will be explicit – this contrasts with the second and heroic direction of the essay: the road taken by the conqueror. Once more the starting-point is lucidity, which leads man to admit that no political miracle can transform the human condition. Yet, while not believing in revolution, the conqueror engages in revolutionary action because the action rather than the goal is valuable. His is an ascetic, masculine code that emphasizes courage and sacrifice. Happiness is set aside in favour of bravery.

If moral thinking has found its way back into the absurd universe, so has politics. When he tells us that he distrusts 'political churches' (167), the conqueror is offering both a criticism of Malraux's Bolshevik man and a hint of Camus's future onslaughts against messianic Marxism. *The Myth* repeats the main political lesson of *Caligula*: that Rome cannot be transformed, and that attempts to do this must end in futile bloodbaths.

When Camus writes in *The Myth* that the 'only concept I can have of freedom is the prisoner's' (140), he is undermining traditional forms of middle-class idealism, as he had done in *The Stranger*. However, while *The Myth* indicates its distrust of all social orders, the most pernicious are those which pretend to absolute legitimacy. The political churches are another form of suicide, and the conqueror is fighting for a revolution that he not merely does not believe in, but also does not want.

The Myth ends by insisting that Sisyphus is happy. In his review Maurice Blanchot argues that, since the absurd lies in the domain of the non-rational, it contains an anguish which cannot be lived with, much less transformed into happiness. For Camus, writes Blanchot, 'the absurd becomes a resolution or a solution' (Maurice Blanchot, 'Le Mythe de Sisyphe', *Faux Pas* (Paris: Gallimard, 1943), p. 70).

This view, which is akin to Sartre's, seems to me correct, as long as it is not taken as a negative criticism. The absurd has become a sort of resolution by acquiring first religious and then moral and political connotations. The stage is now set for the cycle of revolt, where the new values, whether of happiness or of asceticism, will be developed. The sceptical reader may, however, wonder how far such a development can go, since moral and political values cannot take on an independent existence, but remain a part of the static confrontation between man and an absent God. Politically, *The Rebel* opens few perspectives and most of its pages reiterate the attacks on political churches that were made in *The Myth*.

To the reader of *The Stranger* the value of perusing *The Myth* is that it offers additional insights into Part 2. However, these accentuate the difference between the two parts of the novel. In Part 1, the absurd has no coherence and Meursault cannot become aware of it, much less perceive signs in it. In this sense *The Myth* merely highlights the way that *The Stranger* resists interpretation.

Different views of freedom

To discuss the religious aspect of Camus's thought is to assert the difference between him and Sartre. Since the parallels between the two men are obvious but general, whereas the differences are in the long run of greater significance, we shall return to the topic of Camus and religion. But the young Camus and the young Sartre discovered each other as writers of the absurd, even if, as Camus pointed out in the review already quoted, their experience of the absurd was not the same.

They also shared the view that literary French contained an alienation, but the conclusions they drew from this are equally different. Nor are such differences a matter of greater and lesser pessimism. If they were, we might summarize them by saying that Camus was less pessimistic about what man is, and more pessimistic about what he might become.

What Camus and Sartre share is the belief that man's only guide is his direct experience, and that 'others' − parents, bosses and judges − seek to distort that experience in order to subjugate him. This is the conclusion at which *The Stranger* and *Childhood of a Leader* arrive by separate routes. A comparison of these two works is the best way to approach our subject, although we must make a brief detour via *The Wall*, the collection of stories that contains *Childhood*.

In his review of *The Wall*, Camus writes that the stories are case-studies where the characters 'stumble against an absurdity that they cannot overcome' ('*Le Mur* de J.-P. Sartre', *OC* 2,1420). Sartre's heroes and heroines are correct in dismissing the hypocrisy of French society, which is satirized through minor figures like M. Darbédat (*The Room*), who is a patriarch and a paragon of traditional virtues like clarity and precision, and Pierre (*Intimacy*), who incarnates male sexual dominance.

But, if she is right to reject her father, Eve, the heroine of *The Room*, then indulges what Camus calls her 'nostalgia for self-destruction' (*OC* 2,1421). Interpreting *The Wall* via *The Myth*, Camus argues that Eve and Hilbert (*Erostratus*) cannot tolerate the absurd and evade it by flights to madness or, in Hilbert's case, murder.

In a short review Camus cannot deal with the title story, which does not unfold according to the principle of self-destruction. Locked in prison, Pablo tries to confront death lucidly but he is thwarted when he unwittingly betrays a comrade and is released as a reward. To Sartre, Pablo's release is an ironic example of man's lack of control over his existence. The story reveals a sense of human helplessness which is not present in *The Stranger* and which points already to the differences between the two authors. At the same time, however, Pablo had been starting to invent a life in his cell and had been winning the freedom that Sartre would explore in his later books. A similar awareness of freedom is provoked in the reader by *Childhood*, which has a very different hero-narrator.

The relationship between *Childhood* and *The Stranger* emerges from a comparison of the opening lines. *Childhood* begins: '"I am adorable in my little angel suit." Madame Portier had said to mummy: "Your little boy is terribly sweet. He is adorable in his little angel suit"' (*Le Mur* (Paris: Gallimard, 1950 edition), p. 135). Like Meursault, Lucien Fleurié offers us two kinds of language. The first is supposedly his own because it is introduced by an 'I', while the second is the language of others. This is a discourse of banality and affectation — 'terribly sweet' and 'adorable' — and yet the narrator does not criticize it as Meursault criticized the telegram. On the contrary, he adopts it as his own. The 'I' at the outset is ironic because, as the time sequence — 'had said' — reveals, the 'I' stems from the 'your' and the 'he'. Lucien's identity emerges from the words of an 'other', Madame

Portier, who is identified only by her class, for in *Childhood* the designations 'Monsieur' and 'Madame' are reserved for the bourgeoisie.

The definition imposed on the child Lucien troubles him, because the others speak of him as a girl. This provokes a crisis about his body, his sexuality and his relationship with his parents, but he resolves it by further acts of submission. It may seem silly to compare a child-narrator with the adult, Meursault, but Lucien does not change as he grows older. He continues to accept other people's definitions of him and, as a disturbed adolescent, he is relieved when an older man, Bergère, labels his state 'Distress' (170). Once more, his relief is tinged with trouble, ostensibly because he fears the word and the state of 'Distress', but also − so the reader is led to conclude − because he is not living out his own experience.

This is the difference between Lucien and Meursault, who refused other people's notions of love and career, and clung to his existence as he felt it. By contrast, Lucien goes from mentor to mentor in an evolution that takes him through three stages. As a boy he is moulded by his family, which is patriarchal and factory-owning; he rebels in a classically middle-class way and flirts with Freudianism, Surrealism and pederasty; by reaction against such corruption he turns to the far Right, becoming an anti-semite and a follower of the Action Française. This is depicted not as embracing extremism, but as a return to his father's values for, beneath the superficial benevolence with which Monsieur Fleurié runs his factory, lies the reality of power. In *Childhood*, beating up Jews is not very different from giving orders to workers or wives. Lucien lives, then, in inauthenticity; since he is dependent on others, he needs to be feared by them. So, whereas Meursault gradually becomes aware of what separates him from the social and metaphysical order and ends the novel as a rebel, Lucien destroys whatever might be special in him and becomes a man of authority.

A similar difference is present in their attitudes towards language. It has been argued that Meursault distrusts language, whether his own or the state's; Lucien, however, allows himself to be terrorized by it. As a schoolboy he becomes aware of the 'other's' gaze when he sees scrawled on the lavatory wall the phrase 'Lucien Fleurié is gawky' (150). Later he is overawed when a classmate recites a poem he has written according to the Surrealist technique of automatic writing. Far from being a genuine protest against the French of the education system, automatic writing is a deviance that bourgeois society allows because it presents no threat. The proof is that Lucien passes next to the traditional prose of Charles Maurras, the high priest of the Action Française. Once more the circle is complete and *Childhood* has demonstrated not merely that Lucien is a bad reader, but that even in its supposed rebellions French culture is an arm of the ruling class. Lucien enters that class not merely by beating up Jews, but by having his signature printed in the Action Fran-caise newspaper. Now he too participates in what we earlier called the language of authority.

Inevitably, the reader draws further away from Lucien just as he drew closer to Meursault. As narrators, the two play different roles. While the reader feels a barrier between himself and the puzzling narration of Part 1 of *The Stranger*, he is convinced − or almost − by the self-assured irony of Part 2. In *Childhood*, the reader continues to be struck by the falsity of Lucien's narrative. Comedy takes the form not of laughing *with* Lucien, as one laughed with Meursault at the judges, but of laughing *at* both Lucien and his family.

This is achieved by simple devices that increase the reader's distance. *Childhood* presents itself as an inner monologue but, whereas the inner monologue is usually written in the first person and draws the reader into a flux of immediate experience, *Childhood* is written in the third person and its experience is second-hand. The story also has the form of the *roman-à-thèse*, where Lucien is shepherded by a series of role models towards a form of wisdom that is present at the outset. But the models are so unpleasant and the shepherding so obvious that the reader is led to a very different brand of wisdom, namely, the Sartrian concept of freedom that was glimpsed in the title-story. Significantly the quality that is absent from *Childhood* is the one which Sartre considered essential to genuine fiction: the complicity between author and character. *Childhood* invites us to reject it in favour of an unwritten novel where the narration could not be analysed so mechanically.

Since *The Stranger* is fiction and not parody, it is a better piece of writing than *Childhood*. But, if one leaves this aside, the contrasts between the two works give way to similarities. Each defends lived experience against the alienation imposed by the social and cultural order. But this leads us to a further distinction: in *The Wall* authenticity is rarely depicted directly because the absurd cripples the characters. To understand how this is so, we must turn to *Nausea*.

Camus was struck, correctly, by the misery in which Roquentin lives. Whereas Meursault evolves towards a position where he assumes the absurd as a triumph, Roquentin suffers from the collapse of an orderly world view. His inability to control objects or to summon up memories causes him what Blanchot would call anguish. Far from being a defiance of suicide or a reflection of some godhead, the absurd is a debilitating malady.

One of many examples is furnished by the ways Camus and Sartre treat the body. Like Lucien, Roquentin dislikes his body, is convinced of his ugliness and satisfies his sexual needs sordidly. Both Camus and Sartre feel that the body offers certain truths. One remembers how Marie's strong sexuality contrasts with her silly, romantic ideas about love. An episode in *The Age of Reason* (1945) provides the most complete illustration of Sartre's view that the mind invents self-interested fictions, which the body reveals for what they are. In a nightclub, Miss Elinor does a strip-tease, allowing Sartre to dwell on the exploitation of working-class women. But, since Miss Elinor cannot dance, she is unable to disguise the strip-tease as an aesthetic experience; her clumsiness reveals the sexual exploitation and compels the spectators to recognize their voyeurism. This is her body's revenge.

But, if the truth offered by Marie's body is joyful, the message Miss Elinor sends is one of shame. Sartre's treatment of sex rather disgusted Camus and, conversely, Sartre may have felt that Camus's depiction of physical grace was facile. To Sartre there could not be oases of grace that survived amidst the absurd; instead, the human condition as a whole must be transformed. But before examining how this leads to the split between Camus and Sartre, we must consider the problem of language in *Nausea* and *The Stranger*.

Camus criticized the concept of writing exposed in Sartre's closing pages: Roquentin is foolish to imagine that he can save himself by writing a novel. This criticism, which reflects the self-critical narration of *The Stranger*, is correct if one takes Roquentin's statements literally. After the war Sartre himself repeated Camus's rebuke. However, Roquentin never writes the novel he discusses; instead we read a journal which presents itself as incomplete and full of self-criticism. The role of imagination in *Nausea* is to expose Roquentin to the absurd rather than to save him from it. The incident where he imagines that the bar-owner, Fasquelle, is dead is an example of how his imagination offers him correct insights: Fasquelle may not be dead, but the universe is.

This is not in itself an adequate refutation of Camus's criticism, because writing is not a matter of imagination but of words. Yet *Nausea* shows exemplary awareness of how the written language distorts and, like *The Stranger*, it may be read as a criticism of traditional story-telling. Remembering Barthes's interpretation of the gulf between Camus and Balzac, one is not surprised that Roquentin feels a discrepancy between the dialogues of a Balzac novel which he reads in a restaurant and the conversations that are going on around him. But, if the former have a shape that the latter lack, Roquentin rejects such shape as an artifice when, for example, he gives up his biography of Rollebon. He gives up the positivist view that a biographer can know and recreate another person in a book. In a phrase reminiscent of *The Myth* he mentions his need 'to unify my knowledge' (*La Nausée* (Paris: Gallimard, 1983 Folio edition), p. 28), but Rollebon remains an unknowable other. Nor does Roquentin have better success with his journal. From the start he warns himself: 'don't make up exciting things when there's nothing' (11). Soon the journal form breaks down and, as the famous chestnut-tree scene approaches, Roquentin repeats himself, uses long sentences composed almost entirely of main clauses (one remembers Barthes's comment on subordinate clauses), and oscillates between 'I' and 'he'.

The difference between *The Stranger* and *Nausea* is not that Roquentin is saved by writing or that *Nausea* does not criticize itself, but rather that Roquentin ostentatiously reasserts his need to write. Whereas Meursault the narrator hides from the reader − especially in Part 1 − in order to emphasize the problematic of writing, Roquentin flaunts his narrator's role. During the chestnut-tree scene the tree supposedly rids itself of language: 'Things have been freed of their names' (177). But at the end of the scene Roquentin notes 'I left, I came back to the hotel and, there you are, I wrote' (190). The 'there you are' ('et voilà') marks the contradiction.

In his review of *The Stranger*, Sartre rebukes Camus for filtering out of Meursault's experience not merely all idealism but all 'the meaningful connections' which are an integral part of that experience' ('Explication de *L'Etranger*', p. 116). This leaves the novel as a mere assertion of the absurd, and its language as merely reiterating the futility of literary discourse. But this, argues Sartre, is not the point because language, like man himself, is condemned to find meaning. Participating in the absurd, it cannot seek to be neutral or classical. It will become a discourse of liberation and, if no such discourse is present in *Nausea*, it will soon enter Sartre's work.

For Sartre, the absurd is intolerable and man can do nothing but construct out of it a new existence; Camus, however, saw in this another of the leaps of faith that he castigated in *The Myth*. The term 'existentialist' has been used to describe *The Stranger*, and it is legitimate if it is limited to its simplest meaning of the primacy accorded to lived experience. But Camus flatly rejected Existentialism in the Sartrean sense of man's freedom to chose what he would become. In particular, he rejected Sartre's subsequent decision to seek meaning only in history.

A further difference between *Nausea* and *The Stranger* is
that in the former novel the bourgeoisie is present as a class.
In the portrait-gallery scene the burghers of Bouville are set
in their social context; their professions, the events through
which they lived, and the strikes they repressed, are all
depicted. This is a caricature rather than an analysis for, as
in *Childhood*, the bourgeoisie is irredeemably evil. Yet it
forms an easily identifiable target, whereas the ruling class in
The Stranger (which seems to readers of the 1980s a better
novel about how power works in a modern society) is oppressive, because it is amorphous and because its workings
are hard to fathom.

Sartre's view of the bourgeoisie led him, once his interest
in politics was aroused, to the class-war. He took easily to
Marxism and considered violence a necessary part of man's
revolt against his historical situation. By contrast, Camus was
deeply worried about violence and a critic of Marxism.

Yet the quarrel which separated the two men at the height
of the Cold War was not merely between a Sartre who was
anti-American and a Camus who was anti-Soviet. Rather, it
had its roots in *The Stranger* and in Sartre's reaction to it.
Camus, Sartre felt, was complacent about the absurd. Meursault's happiness, the body's grace and the self-critical
language were mystifications; the absurd was intolerable and
the writer's task was to liberate man from it. To Camus,
however, the body's grace was real and should not be sacrific-
ed to an illusory proletarian revolution. Moreover, the absurd
was not intolerable because it was the mark of man's capacity
to be aware of the divine. This religious view, which was
anathema to Sartre, separated the two writers from the
outset. Even Part 1 of *The Stranger*, on which Sartre lavishes
praise, could not altogether satisfy him because, while he ad-
mired its refusal to explain, this refusal could only, he felt, be
a stepping-stone to new forms of freedom.

Chapter 4

Why and how we read *The Stranger*

Contemporaries, precursors and followers

Sartre's article on *The Stranger* helped to make Camus famous, and also to impose a reading of the novel which has remained the dominant reading. In this he was flanked by Blanchot and Barthes, who contributed towards establishing *The Stranger* as the novel of the absurd.

Sartre, whose essay was first published in *Les Cahiers du Sud* in February 1943, stated, as clearly as censorship would allow, the book's meaning to Occupation readers: 'Amidst the literary production of the time this novel was itself a stranger' (J.-P. Sartre, 'Explication de *L'Etranger*', *Situations*, vol. 1 (Paris: Gallimard, 1947), p. 99). Whereas the official culture of Vichy castigated the Third Republic, wept over France's shame and encouraged conformity to the new order, *The Stranger* offered a discourse that stood outside the control of others. The absurd was a refutation of the fictions offered by the Vichy government.

Like Sartre, Blanchot understood that the novel's first quality was a refusal and that Meursault's indifference was a critical, negative force. 'We enter the characters' souls while ignoring the nature of their feelings and thoughts', writes Blanchot, 'this book undermines the concept of subject' (Maurice Blanchot, *Faux Pas* (Paris: Gallimard, 1943), p. 249). Blanchot does not approach the work as joyously as Sartre. He detects in it something of his own anguish – an anguish that is, in his view, too easily banished in *The Myth*.

It was left to Barthes in the post-war years to refine and to alter Sartre's view of *The Stranger*'s refusal to explain. The zero degree of writing that Camus adopted was a moral choice, which rejected the ideology of the ruling class and enabled him to reach 'the existential roots of experience'

(Roland Barthes, *Degré zéro de l'écriture* (Paris: Seuil, 1953), p. 48). Barthes, whose thinking was at this time more obviously Marxist than it subsequently became, argues that, since he was living in a capitalist society, Camus's attempt to write 'neutrally' or 'classically' was doomed to failure. Camus was trapped, and the problematic of *The Stranger*'s language reflected the dilemma of bourgeois culture.

To Barthes, only a change of society would permit a different and freer discourse. In the meantime he distinguished between avant-garde writers like Camus and Marxists like Brecht, whose work contained an awareness that society could be changed. Of course Camus did not accept either this distinction or the concept of a radically different discourse or society. Yet Barthes's analysis of how Meursault's language struggles to avoid causalities and value judgements was persuasive. Barthes's article on the sun ('*L'Etranger*, "roman solaire"' is most easily available in *Les critiques de notre temps et Camus*, edited by Jacqueline Lévi-Valensi (Paris: Garnier Frères, 1970), pp. 60–4) repeated his view that *The Stranger* rejected a false rationalism that was based on power.

So Camus's novel was read as a landmark of the most important trend in 1940s' French thought: the sense that man was trapped in an alien universe, and that he must protest against the artificiality of existing social systems and against his metaphysical condition. In his preface to the English translation, Cyril Connolly, who had read Blanchot's article, called Meursault a 'negative, destructive force', even if he correctly stressed that Meursault was 'profoundly in love with life' (Cyril Connolly, 'Introduction', pp. 11, 8).

As the absurd and Existentialism swept not merely across Saint-Germain but across Europe, *The Stranger* was ever more widely read, inside and outside France. It became such an important part of Western culture not merely because it was a very good novel, but because it incarnated a way of thinking and feeling that was and still is important. This is not necessarily true of great books. A work like Céline's *Fairytale for Another Time*, which seems to me just as good a novel as

The Stranger, has been much less read because it seems marginal to the way most people think and feel. A further reason for *The Stranger*'s success is that it is, superficially, an easy work. This impression is deceptive, but *The Stranger* does not require of the reader the initial effort that Joyce's *Ulysses* requires.

The Stranger's success created distortions, some of which have already been discussed. One has to do with Existentialism: Camus had to keep repeating that his novel was not, in the Sartrean sense, existentialist. Another, which was particularly widespread in the Anglo-Saxon world, was that Meursault was perceived as a hero and that Part 2 was stressed at the expense of the more interesting Part 1. A third was the way that the colonial issue was conveniently forgotten, because Meursault was seen as a universal figure rather than a pied-noir. Camus helped to foster 'easier' and more optimistic interpretations of his novel by his cycle-of-revolt works — which were even more widely read and discussed than *The Stranger* — because readers tended to look in his early writing for the 'positive' moral values that they found in *The Plague.*

We shall return to these topics in our brief examination of the criticism that has been written on *The Stranger*, but first we must set the novel in the history of novel-writing. Although Malraux's *Man's Fate* made such an impact on Camus, the two men had very different ideas of what the novel should be. Indeed, *The Stranger* has no obvious ancestors in French fiction, which led Sartre and many others to wonder whether Camus had not been influenced by the American novel.

Sartre writes that the short, parallel sentences of *The Stranger* are islands like Hemingway's sentences. From there to detecting Hemingway's influence was a short step, and Camus seemed to take it himself. In a 1945 interview he declared that 'I used it [the technique of the American novel] in *The Stranger*, it's true. It suited my purpose, which was to depict a man who seemed to have no awareness' (*OC* 2,1426). When we remember that American novelists were widely read in France and Italy at this time, the case seems proved: *The Stranger* was influenced by *The Sun also Rises.*

The matter is, however, more complex. The question of the American novel is often discussed too loosely, as if every French writer who knew of Hemingway and Faulkner were seeking to emulate them. Their impact should not be treated as mere osmosis, but should be traced through specific milieux. If one conducts such a study in Camus's case, the results are largely negative. His diaries, his journalism and the statements of his friends reveal little contact with American writing. Moreover, the 'tough guy' side of Meursault may more plausibly be attributed to the French-Algerians' view of themselves. Certainly, Camus saw American films and enjoyed imitating Humphrey Bogart, but that does not in itself amount to much.

An American observer, Owen J. Miller ('Camus et Hemingway: pour une évaluation méthodologique', *Albert Camus 4* (Paris: Lettres modernes, 1971)), points out that in the interview Camus revealed scant knowledge of Hemingway since he argued that the American technique reduced men to automatons. This is untrue of Jake Barnes's narration of *The Sun also Rises*, and indeed the difference between this novel and *The Stranger* is precisely that Meursault's narration is less full.

Once more, the first pages reveal the contrast. Where Meursault concludes that the telegram tells him little, Barnes offers a series of speculations about Robert Cohen's wealth and his Jewishness. Although Barnes is undecided about what he thinks of Cohen, this is less a lack of knowledge than a conflict between his dislike of the man and his desire to be generous. Throughout the book Barnes succeeds, in spite of a reticence that is easily explained by pride or masculinity, in telling the reader things about himself: his religion, his impotence and his love for Brett. In short *The Sun also Rises* is − no value judgement is intended − both more of a traditional novel and one where the narrator's terseness contains values that are obviously positive.

Hemingway's novel does explain, and two further contrasts, chosen among many, point to the same underlying difference. The fishing episode in *The Sun* shows Barnes in harmony with nature, whereas Meursault's contact with water and sun is more problematic; Hemingway writes much dialogue, and the banter between Jake and Bill, while seeming inconsequential, reveals male comradeship. By contrast, *The Stranger* contains little dialogue, because Meursault is a lonelier figure who recasts other people's words in free indirect speech.

The parallels are more obvious between *The Stranger* and James M. Cain's *The Postman always Rings Twice*. At his trial, Frank, like Meursault, remains outside the proceedings, forgets to raise his right hand for the oath and laughs with genuine mirth at the magistrate's jokes. But, if here too the conflict lies between Frank's authenticity and society's false values, then both protagonists are presented more directly than in *The Stranger*.

The trial, for example, is simply a piece of manipulation by the insurance companies; Cain shows the capitalist forces lying barely beneath the surface of Californian justice. We are tempted to conclude that the difference between the two novels arises because there is less mystification in American society than in a European and colonial society. This in turn allows the individual to reveal himself. Frank's love of the open road is stressed, the violence of his actions goes beyond the discreet sadism of *The Stranger*, and he feels for Cora a passion that is unlike the desire Meursault feels for Marie. In French-Algeria Meursault must criticize the existing order and must express himself in far more oblique ways.

So it seems to me that the 'influence' of the American novel on *The Stranger* is superficial. I would like to restate the view expressed in Chapters 1 and 2 that, if we wish to define the relationship between *The Stranger* and previous fiction, we should begin by seeing Camus's work as a development and, more importantly, as a criticism of the French journal-novel.

When we turn to the question of Camus's influence on subsequent French writers, we encounter similar difficulties. There are few French novels that resemble *The Stranger*. However, *The Stranger*, as filtered through Sartre's reading, exerted a theoretical influence on the development of French fiction and it was discussed by two theoreticians and practitioners of the new novel. Both Nathalie Saurraute and Alain Robbe-Grillet considered *The Stranger* a precursor of their work. Once more, the ordinary reader sees little in common between Robbe-Grillet's *Jealousy* and *The Stranger*. But Sarraute and Robbe-Grillet argue that, while the French avantgarde of the mid-1950s has relegated the absurd to history, the ways that *The Stranger* criticized the narration, plot, characters and language of the traditional novel influenced their experiments.

Sarraute's thesis is that Camus innovates while reassuring the reader. She stresses the literary aspects of Meursault's discourse: his metaphors and his allusion to his education. She notes that Camus does not follow American novelists in depicting his character from the outside. Rather he does it 'from the inside, by the classic technique of introspection dear to lovers of psychology' (Nathalie Sarraute, *L'Ère du soupçon* (Paris: Gallimard, 1956), p. 15). The use of the journal and the 'I' form comfort the reader, even if they are deployed in non-traditional ways. Indeed, they regain their meaning in Part 2, where Meursault becomes aware of his rebellion.

If we compare this interpretation with Sartre's, we see how the innovations of *The Stranger* have been assimilated. To Sarraute, the novel is a halfway house between traditional fiction and the bolder experiments she is undertaking. Robbe-Grillet expands these insights, first explaining what he likes about *The Stranger*. Anticipating the new novel, it criticizes itself, offers no story and has a main character who is not rounded or convincing.

But to Robbe-Grillet the absence of such things is felt as an anguish, which stems from Camus's residual humanism. The absurd — here Robbe-Grillet could have drawn on *The Myth* — is impossible unless the traditional view of man as the centre of the universe is retained, however dimly. This is the difference, Robbe-Grillet argues, between Camus and the new novel, where objects are looked at for themselves and are not anthropomorphized. The world is 'neither reasonable nor absurd. It is, that's all' (Alain Robbe-Grillet, *Pour un nouveau roman* (Paris: Gallimard, 1964), p. 21).

Robbe-Grillet sees the same regret for a lost human domination in *Nausea* and in Francis Ponge's *The Voice of Things*, where objects are not — despite Ponge's affirmation — depicted for themselves but receive human attributes. In the new novel, so the argument runs, man as master of the universe is not merely no longer present but has never existed.

Further to complicate the matter of Camus's relationship with the next generation of French writers, the new novelists attack the notion of the artist who gives moral and political lessons. This is a repudiation of Camus and Sartre, although chiefly of the post-war Camus and Sartre. By contrast, Robbe-Grillet seems to me correct when he sees in the Camus–Sartre–Ponge debates of the early 1940s the origins of the world view found in the new novel. My only criticism is that he and especially Sarraute underestimate Part 1 of *The Stranger*, which is less reassuring than Part 2.

By the time of Camus's death in 1960, the influence of *The Stranger* had been absorbed by French writers. This does not mean that either the novel or its author ceased to be important to the French avant-garde. After being out of favour in the 1960s, Camus is now fashionable as the critic of Marxism, of the Hegelian view of history and of messianism in general. The new philosophers have read him and use him against Sartre. Whereas French intellectuals of the 1950s generally sided with Sartre during the 1952 quarrel, in the 1980s the victory is retrospectively awarded to Camus. The new philosophers have studied *The Rebel* and they would not accept my earlier comment that it opens few political perspectives.

If *The Stranger* is less important in this context, some of the critical studies it has spurred show that it anticipated certain trends in what might vaguely be called left-wing thinking. As stated in Chapters 2 and 3, it shows that power is amorphous and creates an alienation that pervades society; opposed social groups find it difficult to explain much less to combat their situation. This view — along with such developments as the impossibility of general revolt, the refusal of a rationality that is deemed spurious and a scepticism about language — crops up in the later Barthes, in Foucault and elsewhere.

Finally we must restate — at the risk of being banal — that *The Stranger's* importance does not come from its appeal to a French avant-garde. Rather, it lies in the way that the novel has caught fundamental traits of modern individualism: the determination to trust one's own experience while distrusting the many and varied forms of authority, the attempt to face the absence of transcendence and to enjoy this life, and the recognition that it is difficult to use language to say even the simplest things.

Suggestions for further reading

Readers who wish to know more of why and how *The Stranger* is read may consult some of the works that have been written on it. No attempt can be made here to describe or even to list the enormous number of books and articles in which the novel is analysed. For such information the reader may consult the work of Brian T. Fitch and Peter C. Hoy. Fitch offers an excellent bibliography at the end of his book *'L'Etranger' d'Albert Camus, un texte, ses lecteurs, leurs lectures* (Paris: Librairie Larousse, 1972). Fitch and Hoy are the co-authors of *Calepins de bibliographie: Albert Camus 1* (Paris: Lettres modernes, 1972), which lists French-language studies of Camus published up to 1970. Articles and books, whether in English or French, are regularly noted in the Revue des Lettres modernes series on Camus (see below), which is edited by Fitch. All that is attempted here is to mention some of the milestones in criticism of *The Stranger*, to review the English translations and to comment on the film.

In the Anglo-Saxon world, Camus's audience is especially wide. Anglo-Saxons have always tended to support him against Sartre, to approve his critique of Marxism and to admire his concern — which seems to them characteristically French — for moral values. Three books were especially influential in disseminating his thought: Germaine Brée's *Camus* (New Brunswick: Rutgers University Press, 1959); John Cruickshank's *Albert Camus and the Literature of Revolt (Oxford University Press, 1960); Philip Thody's Camus* (London: Hamish Hamilton, 1958). All three have sections on *The Stranger*, which they place in the evolution of Camus's work and, since all three are clearly written, they have attracted a non-specialist as well as a specialist audience.

Another influential text was a preface written by Camus himself for an American edition of *The Stranger* (reproduced *OC* 1,1928), which stresses Meursault's passion for truth. Although Camus warns against idealizing Meursault, this piece, which depicts Meursault as the individual persecuted by society, while ignoring his alienation, his working-class roots and the way he ridicules idealism, could lead the reader to consider Meursault a hero or a martyr.

At least one observer struggled against interpretations that ignored the troubling aspects of the novel (René Girard, 'Camus' Stranger revisited', *PMLA*, December 1964, pp. 519 – 33). But there was in Anglo-Saxon culture a tendency either to discover positive values in Meursault or else to lament the absence of them. Either way, the incomplete and critical qualities of Meursault's discourse were somewhat neglected. This tendency was accentuated by Stuart Gilbert's translation, which makes *The Stranger* a rather more comfortable novel than *L'Etranger*.

Readers paid little attention to the colonial theme until the advent of decolonization and the furious debates about the Algerian War which saddened Camus's last years. In 1943 Sartre did not dwell on the murder of the Arab, although Cyril Connolly discusses it in his preface. In the 1960s *The Stranger* became politically controversial, and Conor Cruise O'Brien expressed doubts about the way Camus handled the murder. Both Meursault's indifference to the beating up of the Arab woman and the depiction of the legal system were criticized by O'Brien. No French court would have condemned Meursault for the murder of an armed Arab, O'Brien argues, so the image of Meursault, the rebel, is unreal (C. C.

O'Brien, *Albert Camus*, London: Fontana/Collins, 1970).

Since the 1960s the colonial issue has remained a motif in Camus studies. Much research has been done on the French-Algeria of the 1930s and here the best starting-point is the edition of Camus's *Alger-Républicain* journalism: *Fragments d'un combat, Cahiers Albert Camus 3*, edited by Jacqueline Lévi-Valensi and André Abbou (Paris: Gallimard, 1978).

Readers interested in this theme may also trace it through Camus's later books and may linger over the early pages of *The Plague*. The journalist, Rambert, comes to Algeria to do an article on the Arab question, but he never writes it. This is another enigmatic episode where the unwritten text lingers as an absence alongside the many texts – Tarrou's journal, Paneloux's sermons and Rieux's narrative – that constitute the novel. In *The Exile and the Kingdom* Camus could deal more openly with the issue because the Arab rebellion had clarified the relationship between colonizer and colonized. It is also interesting to compare his insights into colonialism with those of Conrad, Forster and Orwell.

But the main body of recent criticism of *The Stranger* deals quite properly with its language, structure and narrative technique. Two excellent studies of the way Meursault tells his story are M.-G. Barrier's *L'Art du récit dans 'L'Etranger'* (Paris: Nizet, 1962) and Brian T. Fitch's *Narrateur et narration dans 'L'Etranger' d'Albert Camus* (Paris: Minard, 1968)). The Minard Lettres modernes series of Camus volumes, edited by Fitch, begins with a number devoted to *The Stranger* (*Autour de 'L'Etranger'*, *Albert Camus 1* (Paris: Revue des Lettres modernes, 1968). The whole series is of special importance to students of literary criticism. Such readers will also enjoy Uri Eisenzweig's *Les Jeux de l'écriture dans 'L'Etranger' de Camus* (Paris: Lettres modernes, 1983), which draws on Derrida's thought to analyse the various kinds of language in the novel.

Literary theory has been spurred by *The Stranger* and may also help to explicate it. Here, my choice is inevitably arbitrary and I shall do no more than mention two texts that may be helpful in accounting for Part 1, Chapter 6: Michel

Foucault's *L'Ordre du discours* (Paris: Gallimard, 1971) and Pierre Macherey's *Pour une théorie de la production littéraire* (Paris: Maspéro, 1966).

Of the many studies of different aspects of *The Stranger* several may be – once more arbitrarily – cited. In Chapter 2, an argument is made against the notion that Meursault may be seen as a pagan, but it is only fair to note that many readers disagree. A good defence of their view is Robert Champigny's *Sur un héros païen* (Paris: Gallimard, 1959). An article on the important subject of ambiguity is Brian Fitch's 'Le paradigme herméneutique chez Camus', in *Albert Camus*, edited by Raymond Guy-Crosier (Gainsville: University of Florida Press, 1980). This whole volume is mainstream academic criticism. Carl A. Viggiani's article 'Camus' *L'Etranger*', *PMLA*, December 1956, pp. 865–87, is a suggestive interpretation of the novel's ending. For the language used in Part 1, Chapters 1 and 6, a good place to start is Stephen Ullmann's 'The two styles of Camus', in *The Image in the Modern French Novel* (Cambridge: Cambridge University Press, 1960), pp. 236–99. A computer-based study of the colours in *The Stranger*, which also shows how useful computers can be in literary criticism, is Robin Adamson's 'The colour vocabulary in *L'Etranger*', *Association for Literature and Linguistics Computer Bulletin*, vol. 7, no. 3, pp. 221–37.

Biographical information is given in abundance in Herbert Lottman's *Albert Camus, a Biography* (New York: Doubleday, 1979). In particular Lottman gives many details about the publication of *The Stranger*.

The psychoanalytical approach to the novel is fruitful, and I have drawn heavily on Jean Gassin's *L'Univers symbolique d'Albert Camus* (Paris: Minard, 1981).

Finally, for the general reader who does not wish to tackle the Lettres modernes series there are several guides to *The Stranger* that are written in clear, simple language. They include K. R. Dutton's *Camus' 'L'Etranger': From Text to Criticism* (Macquarie University, 1976), G. V. Banks's *Camus' 'L'Etranger'* (London: Edward Arnold, 1976), Rosemarie Jones's Camus: *'L'Etranger' and 'La Chute'*

(London: Grant and Cutler, 1980) and Adele King's *Notes on 'L'Etranger'* (London: Longman, York Press, 1980). There is also an edition of the French text with useful notes for the Anglo-Saxon reader: *L'Etranger*, edited by Germaine Brée and Carlos Lynes (London: Methuen, 1958).

Translations

Stuart Gilbert's translation is partially responsible for *The Stranger*'s success in the Anglo-Saxon world (Albert Camus, *The Outsider* (Hamish Hamilton, 1946, Penguin 1961); references are to the Penguin edition). Gilbert's merit was to offer a clear version that flows well. If he may be criticized, it is because, while *L'Etranger* does not explain, his translation does.

One should of course remember that he was translating the original 1942 version and that Camus made at least two revisions: in 1947 and between 1949 and 1953. In general the changes increased the concision of the novel, which is another reason why one should hesitate before criticizing Gilbert. Two such changes are of interest in themselves. Camus took out a statement that Meursault masturbated in prison: 'Next day I did like the others' (Gilbert, p. 80). Missing, too, is a concluding, poetic sentence of Part 1, Chapter 3: 'through the sleep-bound house the little plaintive sound rose slowly like a flower growing out of the silence and the darkness' (Gilbert, p. 41). The reference to the flower reminds us of the geraniums on the mother's grave and makes the links among her, the Arab woman and Salamano's dog more explicit, while the metaphorical language invites us to see connections between Chapter 3 and Chapters 1 and 6 of Part 1.

Gilbert was, then, translating a slightly fuller version of *L'Etranger*, but he may still be said to elaborate on it more than he need have done. He makes a few mistakes: the Arab nurse's smock becomes 'blue' (Gilbert, p. 16), which falsifies the colour scheme. More importantly, he shrinks from the sexual frankness of 'j'ai eu très envie d'elle' and uses the euphemism 'I couldn't take my eyes off her' (p. 41). Gilbert seems ill at ease with the earthy, working-class flavour of *The Stranger*.

But he is even less at ease with its remoteness. He renders 'Emmanuel riait à perdre haleine' by 'Emmanuel chuckled, and panted in my ear, "we've made it"' (p. 34). There is no reason to add a piece of direct speech by Emmanuel who belongs to the segment of the working class that least trusts language.

Substitution of direct for indirect and free indirect speech is the gravest fault in the translation. Céleste gives his evidence in indirect speech but Gilbert renders it by direct speech (p. 93), ignoring the theme that Céleste is not being allowed by the court to say what he would like to say. In Part 1, Chapter 3, Gilbert turns many of Raymond's utterances into direct speech, such as 'You've knocked around the world a bit and I dare say you can help me. And then I'll be your pal for life; I never forget anyone who does me a good turn' (p. 37). Gilbert seems to have added a phrase here too, but it is more important that by letting Raymond speak directly he is increasing the authenticity of Raymond's friendship for Meursault. This is a complex matter because, as I argued in Chapter 2, there is more direct speech in this episode than elsewhere. But it is surely wrong to increase the amount, because the presence of indirect speech also enables the reader to maintain a certain distance from Raymond.

Distance is less of a theme in the English text and Gilbert seems uncertain of how to handle Meursault's 'I think' and 'I believe'. When for once they are omitted by Camus, he inserts them. When Meursault writes 'Maman, sans être athée, n'avait jamais pensé de son vivant à la religion', Gilbert translated by 'So far as I knew, my mother . . .' (p. 15). But this is − as has also been argued − a moment of ostentatious omniscience that draws our attention to Meursault's agnosticism.

Joseph Laredo's new translation (Hamish Hamilton, 1982, Penguin, 1983; references are to the Penguin edition) is more faithful to the difficulties of the text. Laredo corrects Gilbert's mistakes and gets the balance between direct and indirect speech right. He does not try to blur the discrepancies in the time sequence on the opening page. In general, his tone is franker and more colloquial than Gilbert's. He translates the 'j'ai eu très envie d'elle' by 'I really fancied her' (p. 37); where Gilbert uses 'one' Laredo tends to use 'you', and when Raymond says 'copain' Laredo renders it by 'mate' (p. 33). Gilbert gratuitously inserts 'old boy' into Raymond's speech, but Laredo omits it.

His translation has a working-class tone that is present in the French and that also accentuates, by contrast, the intellectual quality of Meursault's language. Precisely because it is more colloquial, Laredo's version is British and not American, which may explain why a new American translation by Mathew Ward is scheduled to be published by Knopf in 1987.

Lo Straniero

It remains to note the film of the novel: *Lo Straniero*, 1967, directed by Luchino Visconti with Marcello Mastroianni as Meursault and Anna Karina as Marie. Although Visconti might seem, because of his ties with neo-realism and with the Italian Communist Party, well able to interpret the colonial aspect of *The Stranger*, he fails to do so, except in one good scene where Meursault arrives in prison to find himself surrounded by Arabs, one of whom plays the flute.

More importantly, Visconti is unable to find a cinematic language to render Meursault's puzzling narration. The best scene in the film shows the funeral procession struggling along the road while Pérez darts through the fields. Both the futility of mourning and Pérez's authenticity are rendered. But one can only wonder why Visconti did not attempt to match the seeming neutrality of Meursault's discourse by letting the camera move silently over the Algiers streets or over the objects in Meursault's flat.

As a critic of Visonti's work has put it, the director 'crowds out the silence with a host of unnecessary and obtrusive presences' (Geoffrey Nowell-Smith, *Luchino Visconti*, 2nd edn (New York: Viking Press, 1973), p. 184). Indeed, Visconti provides the information that Camus withheld, giving us Meursault's first name — Arthur — and his date of birth — 1903. Mastroianni is too expressive in his gestures and grimaces (Visconti would have preferred Alain Delon, who is more of a tough guy), and Anna Karina, while suitably sexy, is too much a tragic heroine during the trial scene.

Visconti does stress the Algiers and working-class surroundings, while the scenes with Raymond are good. But even the shots of the port clutter the film and remind us that *The Stranger* is not a realist novel and that figurative detail — like the advertisement for Bastos cigarettes — cannot replace the clash of languages that lies at the core of the novel, and that could surely be rendered by a different kind of cinema. Should there not be another film of *The Stranger*?